The Journey of a Lifetime

Travel with an evangelist's daughter through miracles, disappointments, and the unknown...

Rachelle Michal Mann, B.S., M.A.T.

The Journey of a Lifetime

"When He Was on the Cross" *Michael Payne & Ronny Hinson* ~ Lyrics used by permission.

"Even When You're Asking Why" *Mike Bowling, Kelly Bowling & Marcia Henry* ~ Lyrics used by permission.

Printed at:
Pollock Printing Company
Nashville, TN

Editing: Victoria R. Mann & Rev. David L. Mann
Photography & Graphic Design: David J. Mann

The Journey of a Lifetime

Dedication

 This book is dedicated to Eric Bennett – a minister of the gospel, an outstanding bass singer, and a dear friend. Your genuine encouragement and heartfelt advice sparked my zeal and determination to share my story. Thank you for inspiring me to write this book! You were truly the key influence in making this dream a reality. I am so grateful the Lord allowed our paths to cross, and I will always cherish your friendship.

Contents

Foreword

Great things happen when you truly put your faith and trust in God and believe with Him all things are possible. I was so encouraged by this book. I'm a Huge Rachelle Mann Fan, and I feel the best is yet to come on her journey.

Scotty Inman
Gospel Artist with Triumphant Quartet

Our family had the privilege to open our home to Rachelle while she was a student teacher in Tennessee. What a blessing she was, bringing her warm spirit and a love that is so evident for Christ. She won our hearts immediately. I know you will be encouraged as she tells her story of being a girl that has grown up in ministry traveling the country with her family. You will feel her pure heart on each page and be reminded that "salt of the earth" people do still exist.

Kelly Bowling
Gospel Artist with The Bowling Family

My wife Marsha and I have known Rachelle's parents, David and Victoria, for more than thirty years. We have known Rachelle and "little David" all their lives! We recall the early days, when this tiny little girl with long flowing naturally curly red hair would stand on the platform and sing just before her daddy preached! From the time she first learned to talk, she hasn't stopped talking and singing about her love for Jesus. Now, an honors college graduate, certified teacher, gifted musician, Nashville recording artist, and author. Rachelle Mann strives to excel in every thing she does to the Glory of God! This book is the story of a life wholly dedicated to serving Jesus Christ!

Marcus Alexander, Ph.D.
Lead Pastor of Casa View Assembly

How blessed we feel at the Christian Church of Bayonne to see our youth hungering after the Lord and serving Him with such a love and desire. These blessings multiplied when Rachelle Mann came into our church families' lives. We have been truly blessed to have her minister every summer at our youth retreats at Refreshing Mountain. God has been so amazing how He has used Rachelle to serve and minister to them through Bible devotionals and worship. Through Rachelle's

Christian example and obedience to God's will, we have seen lives changed, transformed, and inspired to also preach the Word of God. Friendships that will last a lifetime have been sparked through God's unity and love.

Lydia Megale, M.M.E.
Pastor's wife at Christian Church of Bayonne

You must read!!! Such a heart for Jesus. This book will change your life.

Jason Crabb
Gospel Artist

The Journey of a Lifetime

Introduction

    Living an unusual life is a magnet for questions of all kinds. People frequently ask what it is like to live on a bus, travel full-time, meet new people, minister in all types of churches, and get along with each other in only 382 square feet of living space. The question topics range from miraculous faith-building experiences to our favorite places to eat across the nation. Friends, acquaintances, and strangers alike have expressed their curiosity about the pros and cons of being a full-time evangelist family. Over the years, we have told countless personal stories of unexpected miracles, awkward moments, special family memories, and incredible times in God's presence. Our experiences also include being resented by family members, lied about by friends, and overwhelmed by the struggles of life. We have waded through deep valleys of pain, watched relationships disintegrate, and witnessed alarming changes…all the while determined to emerge victorious with God's help.

    Indeed, the highlights of life on the road are innumerable, and the challenges are as well. I could never recall or have space enough to include all the experiences that an amazing God and nearly twenty-three years of traveling have composed. Nevertheless, my goal in this book is to lead you through some of the valleys and over some of the mountaintops that I have encountered during my journey of a lifetime.

To protect the privacy and integrity of individuals, I have omitted or changed the names of people who are not immediate family. Also, I have left locations anonymous or limited location descriptions to states.

The Journey of a Lifetime

Chapter 1

A Journey's Beginning

It all began in a country town nestled among the foothills of California's Sierra Nevada Mountains. January of 1992 offered an inviting ministry opportunity for a young couple. David and Victoria Mann, who had been happily married for about eighteen months, accepted a youth pastor position at a small church in northern California. They moved into a two-bedroom rental home just a few blocks from the church and poured their lives into the adolescents who attended the activities and services the church provided. Some of the youth were from drug homes, some were from broken families, and some were "church kids." But each one found a place in the hearts of David and Victoria, and with all their might, these dedicated youth pastors reached to the home-town mission field of hopeless youngsters.

Meanwhile, three years of youth pastoring were full of other ventures for the young couple. David worked at his stepdad's optical business, and

11

Victoria taught at a private elementary school. During the summers of 1992 and 1993, David and Victoria were both able to take several months off work. Because of their heart for the ministry, the young couple used these vacation opportunities for going on evangelistic tours to the eastern United States. They would cram their luggage into the trunk of a 1987 Thunderbird and head east to preach revivals and special services. New destinations in mission-field America were tugging on the heart strings of the young couple. Whatever doors opened, wherever God directed, David and Victoria were willing to go. Soon, hitting the road every few days, living out of suitcases, ministering in different churches, and meeting new people somehow began to feel normal. Nevertheless, at the close of each summer, the young couple would return to their country home in California and settle back into their vocational routines. And of course, David and Victoria were eager to resume their dedicated work with the youth of their town.

In October of 1993, life brought special delight when David and Victoria found out they were expecting their first child. As the young couple shared the news with their relatives, excitement escalated considerably because the baby would be the first grandchild and first great grandchild for David's family. Yet excitement quickly faded into concern and disappointment in November when Victoria began having major complications with her pregnancy. The doctors advised bed rest and seriously warned David and Victoria to prepare for the worst. A miscarriage seemed inevitable. Nevertheless, David and Victoria kept their faith in God Who could work all things for the good of those who love Him and are called according to His purpose (Romans 8:28). Also, fellow believers were agreeing with the young couple in prayer for a divine intervention. Indeed, the miraculous was their only hope, and a miracle was exactly what the young couple was believing God to perform.

Victoria spent Thanksgiving in bed with family gathered around trying to help make the most of the holiday festivities under the distressing circumstances. The following day, another phone conversation with the doctor revealed that there was no hope of the baby's survival, and if the situation worsened, David should take Victoria to the emergency room for her physical safety. Sunday morning dawned to the grim reality that Victoria's complications persisted and that the baby had likely passed away. David was preparing to attend Sunday morning service by himself when he felt the Holy Spirit instructing him to ask the elders of the church to come over for prayer. After church, the pastor and his wife as well as a board member and his wife arrived at David and Victoria's little home to, once again, petition Heaven for a miracle. David laid Victoria on their couch, and the elders gathered around. During a powerful time of intercessory prayer in that humble living room, the Holy Spirit declared these words: "I have not spoken death, but I have spoken life." David and Victoria rejoiced in that message of life they received from the Lord.

Monday morning brought continued encouragement as Victoria's complications began to improve. When the young couple arrived at their pre-scheduled doctor's appointment, they were clinging to the thread of hope that God had proclaimed, despite apparent circumstances and negative diagnoses from professionals. Concerned by the pregnancy complications that Victoria had been experiencing, the doctor and nurses frantically asserted that they needed to perform several tests on Victoria. Nevertheless, David and Victoria felt at peace about the situation, so they refused the tests and returned home, believing that God would be faithful to His promise.

Through the trying weeks of a troubled pregnancy, the young couple learned the importance of trust, the power of prayer, and the unfailing nature of God. Indeed, the Almighty proved to be faithful, and on June 21, 1994, David and Victoria's new addition to the family arrived, a healthy baby girl named Rachelle Michal Mann. Though the devil tried to end my journey before it began, the Master had greater plans. The Holy Spirit's promise of life, given months before, was fulfilled, and my journey's beginning was a miracle moment that only God could have performed.

During the following months, my parents were busy with what might be considered ordinary responsibilities: youth ministry, work, and parenting. We still lived in the small rental home a few blocks from the country church. My daddy continued working at his parents' business, and my momma stayed home to care for me. Together, we attended the church where my parents were youth pastoring. That first year of my life seemed to be typical for a young, Christian family, at least in the eyes of society. Little did we know, that would be our family's only so-called "normal" year. The Lord was about to put a plan into effect that would alter the course of my life. Our world was going to be drastically changed.

As the summer of 1995 approached, my dad began praying for direction concerning another East Coast ministry trip. Several doors began opening for revivals and services. However, as my parents prepared for a summer tour, God started nudging them to take a much larger step of faith.

The idea of full-time evangelism began flooding their minds and resounding through their hearts. My parents intently pondered the ramifications, but the possible outcomes of that "traveling full-time" notion were endless. Some thoughts were exciting; some were frightening. My dad had a wife and daughter to provide for, and full-time evangelism meant there would be no weekly salary, no stationary home, no security of a stable bank account, and no guarantee of a predictable schedule. (Not much has changed in 23 years!) What if the ministry doors closed after two months on the road? What if the bills surpassed the income? What if there was no place to go between engagements? What if…? What would happen if they went full-time? My parents had no answers to these questions and uncertainties.

Discouragement poured in from unlikely sources. Fellow Christians advised my parents that they could not make it on the evangelistic field. And besides, their children would suffer and be socially inept. Full-time evangelism was just not an appropriate occupation for the late twentieth century. Life on the road was too hard and not financially sufficient to support a family. These skeptical counselors even told my daddy that prayer, dedication, and preaching would not affect God's outpouring of revival. Instead, God just sends revival whenever and wherever He decides to; individual efforts have nothing to do with it.

Nevertheless, both my mom and dad had a heart for ministry, particularly for the evangelistic field. Traveling to minister in all different types of churches and reaching for people all across mission-field America were driving desires deep in my parents' hearts that they dared not stifle. And those feelings of normality and contentment they experienced in previous years during their summer evangelistic trips began to grip their hearts afresh. The opportunities to share the gospel, the countless individuals needing hope, the pathway God was paving, and the adventure that awaited…it was a calling that captured my parents.

Soon, the thoughts of stepping out in faith seemed to overwhelmingly overtake the thoughts of fear and doubt. Regardless of the skeptical counsel, the unavoidable obstacles, and the possibility of failure, God was calling, and that was an undeniable fact for my parents. If God called, He would equip. If God equipped, my mom and dad knew that they could fulfill a divine mission of full-time evangelism.

Resolve, passion, and trust were motivating factors that pressed my parents toward their sure calling. And by the end of May 1995, my daddy had given a thirty-day notice to his family's business and to the owner of our cozy rental home. Also, my parents spoke with the pastor about their plans to step down from their youth pastorate position at the church.

Since they had lunged forward in utter dependence on God, my dad imagined that pastors would start calling to schedule revival meetings. A final, unexpected test came when the phone did ring, and our first revival canceled. Despite this thrust of discouragement, my parents kept clinging to the dream of full-time evangelistic ministry, even though their calendar only revealed a two-month itinerary. Instead of giving up, my mom and dad had solidified their faith, overcome their reservations, disregarded the skeptics, and agreed to wholeheartedly play their part in putting God's plan into action. Whether the culmination would be tragedy or triumph was for God to decide, but now, there was no looking back.

The coming weeks were filled with moving treasured belongings to storage, giving away items that were unneeded, and packing essentials. My family was about to change residency from a 1,000 square-foot house to a two-door, extra-cab, Ford pick-up with a camper shell. As a result, the preparations to step into full-time ministry on the road were very involved. By June 21, the packing process was nearly complete, and my first birthday was the final holiday we celebrated in that little, country home. Surrounded by boxes of our possessions, we used a table and folding chairs from our church as furniture for the party. Those final special moments in my stationary home faded into memories, and the day of our departure, June 29, quickly arrived.

Soon, my parents were packing our belongings in the truck bed and climbing into the front seat of the blue and white Ford. My daddy took his place behind the steering wheel, my mommy sat on the passenger side, and I fit perfectly between my parents on the bench seat. After bidding a final farewell to our relatives, our dear friends, our little home, and our country town, we hit the road, headed east to Illinois on our first venture as a full-time evangelist family. Our journey's beginning was a radical step of faith to pursue a God-given calling that would transform our lives.

Wherever God opened the doors, we were eager to share the gospel. From the swamps of Louisiana to the corn fields of Indiana and from crowded cities in New England states to country towns in California, our family ministered at youth camps, special services, and revivals. We even ventured north to Ontario, Canada for a ministry opportunity in a Jamaican church. During that inaugural tour of full-time evangelism, we stayed with pastors or parishioners who graciously opened their homes to our family of three. In between scheduled meetings, we would spend a few days with relatives in New Jersey or Indiana. Then for those nights on the road, a foam mattress in the backseat of our pick-up served as the perfect bed for Momma and me. If my dad decided to pull over and rest, he lay on the front bench seat of our truck to sleep. We frequented rest areas, Flying J truck stops, and Walmart parking lots all over the United States. And strangely, those highways that stretched across America seemed more and more like home.

Months flew by as we racked up the miles on the odometer of that blue and white Ford. By the winter of 1995, we headed back to California where we spent the Christmas holiday with relatives. Then, my parents and I stayed with family for a few months because my mom was expecting another baby. Throughout late winter and early spring, we traveled and ministered locally while we awaited the arrival of our newest addition. On April 25, 1996, David Joshua Mann was born. That special day added the final member to the *Mann Clan*, and our ministry journey as an evangelist family of four officially began.

During those first months of traveling in the

blue and white pick-up, I sat in my car seat between my parents as we journeyed across America. While we drove, my daddy and momma would talk to me, ask me questions, and prompt me to respond or to imitate their words. Consequently, as a two-year-old girl, I was quite vocal and inquisitive. After nearly a year of living out of a truck and staying with other people, I began to notice that I did not have a home. Approaching my momma with a list of questions, I first asked about one of my playmates: "Where is Sarah?" Mom explained to me that Sarah was at her home. I quickly blurted out a second question about another friend: "Where is Jackie?" My young momma patiently told me that Jackie was at her home. I responded with a third question that was more personal to me and to my mother: "Where is Rachelle's home?" As a two-year-old child, I had discovered in a simple yet profound sense that my life was not normal. I did not have a home like the other little girls I knew.

When we left our home in California to be on the road full-time, critics told my parents that my brother and I would suffer as a result of the atypical lifestyle that my parents chose. Nevertheless, my daddy and momma put their trust in the Lord. If He called us to ministry, He would faithfully provide for every aspect of life. When I began questioning my mom about a home, she suddenly realized that I had a personal need, even as a toddler.

Now let me note that during this type of moment, the devil tries desperately to place doubt in the minds of God's children. *Possibly those critics were right. Your daughter is only two years old, and she is already questioning her abnormal lifestyle. Maybe your children will suffer socially and mentally from being "different."* Of course, the devil may not have whispered those exact words to my mom, but he often uses similar sly tactics in an attempt to weaken the faith of believers. Yet we are not ignorant of Satan's devices; he plays dirty (2 Corinthians 2:11). Consequently, we must be on guard against the devil's strategies, believing instead that God will always be faithful to His Word.

Perhaps the devil meant for my inquisition about a home to be a moment in which my mom questioned the validity of God's calling on her life and the certainty of His faithfulness to her children. However, my parents were well familiar with the devil's desperate efforts to deter them from the ministry that the Lord had called them to fulfill. Even in the face of criticism, obstacles, and doubt, my parents had already chosen the year before to move forward into God's plan for their lives. This new question that I had unexpectedly proposed to my momma would simply be another opportunity for my parents to trust that God knew what He was doing, even when the devil and the circumstances seemed to say otherwise.

Once again, God proved the critics wrong and discounted Satan's lies when in response to my question about a place to live, my mom was able to assure me that we were getting a home. My parents had already ordered a travel trailer and Suburban to be our new home on wheels. The Lord confirmed to my parents that He was taking care of my need before they were even aware it existed. Clearly, God had their back!

In May of 1996, the exciting day arrived that my daddy drove a 1990, blue and white, Chevy Suburban into the driveway of my grandparents' house. Hitched to the back of the Suburban was a 33-foot Sunnybrook travel trailer. It was home sweet home. The white aluminum siding, decorated with wispy blue stripes, glimmered in the sunlight. I eagerly ran inside, touching the pieces of furniture as I completed my first tour and claiming them as "Rachelle's couch," "Rachelle's table," and so on. When I reached the bedroom in the back of the trailer, I clarified that the bed belonged to Daddy and Momma. Then I patted the floor in the bedroom, and with sincere satisfaction, I labeled it "Rachelle's bed." My journey in a home on wheels had begun as a demonstration of God's provision for my need and a landmark of His faithfulness.

Our Chevy Suburban was transportation for thousands of miles on interstates, turnpikes, and country roads all across America, and the Sunnybrook trailer was home in whatever state we parked it. Soon, traveling full-time for over three years gave me the identity of an evangelist's daughter. Furthermore, hearing my father minister approximately two hundred times each year was sufficient to identify me as a preacher's kid. However, it was that precious revival service in the late winter of 1999 that truly changed my life. I still remember kneeling on the brown-carpeted step at the front of a rustic, hillside church in California. As tears streamed down my face and the Savior's blood cleansed my heart, I received a new identity. At that moment, I was transformed into a child of the King. Truly, the greatest journey I have ever embarked upon began when Christ became my life and Heaven became my destination.

The Journey of a Lifetime

Chapter 2

He Made a Way

~∽◯∾~

Although we had just started a tent revival in Missouri, that unforgettable Tuesday evening was not the ideal setting for an outdoor service. The overcast sky was a dreadful combination of charcoal gray, deep purple, and forest green. Harsh winds swept billowing clouds swiftly across the horizon as if they were late to a serious appointment. All too soon, the frightening storm clouds were dumping rain, and the shrill of an eerie siren echoed a grim warning throughout the little town. A tornado had touched down several miles away, and now, we were the next victims in its path.

The pastor frantically knocked on our bus door to advise my dad that we should take refuge in the brick section of the church building. Since the weather was getting scary, we hurried over to shelter. My brother and I were just young kids huddled on the floor of the church's brick annex with Mom staying close by. Church members who had already arrived for the scheduled service were sitting in the room with us. Meanwhile, my dad was standing just outside the back door with the pastor and associate pastor. The three men were watching the storm's progression and praying for God to intervene. Suddenly, the associate pastor yelled, "It's dropping!" Above the church property, a tornado funnel had formed out of the churning storm clouds, and it started falling toward the ground. My dad and the pastors began interceding fervently for a miracle. Then as abruptly as the twister began dropping, it lost its force and disintegrated. Directly overhead where the tornado once was, the clouds split to reveal clear, blue sky. I can still picture what it looked like for the storm clouds to engulf the horizon as far as the eye could see with the exception of a blue hole right above the church. We had service inside the sanctuary that evening, and the weather gave us no problem that night or the rest of the revival. God came through for us. His protection was evident. He made a way.

This was not the first time I watched God intervene in a situation that seemed impossible, neither was it the last. Being on the road for over twenty-two years has generated many experiences that each required divine involvement. I am not saying that it is always easy to have faith that everything will work out when peril, debt, or sickness is staring you in the face. But what I am saying is that God never fails to come through in

His timing. He has pulled us out of financial straits, provided for our needs, and protected us from danger…more times than I could count. So I will take you along to just a few milestones on my journey that reveal His faithfulness to make a way.

After three years and thousands of miles, our well-worn Sunnybrook trailer had seen better days. It was made for camping in – not for living in and dragging all across the United States. So the Lord provided for us to purchase a 40-foot fifth-wheel and a truck to tow our new home. This trailer had two bedrooms, which meant that David and I got to have a bedroom with bunkbeds. In the living room area, there was enough space for a keyboard and eventually a small drum set too…life was never quiet!

Anyways, we made lots of memories in the fifth-wheel. Like the fateful summer when our air conditioner quit working in Arkansas in July! I am telling you, that trailer was like a slow cooker. We survived with a window unit keeping the daytime temperature slightly under one hundred degrees for a week or two until we could get our AC repaired. Or the time when the town we were ministering in had a plague of slimy, green tree frogs…three of which decided to uninvitedly take up residence in the trailer. Of course, once we found the critters, we quickly terminated their stay, but Mom's discovery of such occupants in our home was *not* calm. Then there were the experiences of falling out of bed from the top bunk. One night I woke up on the way down, grabbing for the sheets and blankets to catch myself, which turned out to be a pointless effort. Okay, somehow I got non-spiritual very quickly. However, I will say this: amidst all the memories, the five and a half years that we pulled that second trailer from coast to coast was a constant reminder of God's provision for our need.

We were making one of our final trips with the fifth-wheel, and as usual, I was riding in the backseat of the truck. I was a 10-year-old girl, very accustomed to spending hours on the road. To make the hours pass, sometimes I did school work. Sometimes I played with my toys. And sometimes I stared out the window. On this particular travel day, I was peering through the back window when I noticed that the trailer did not look quite right. It seemed to be rickety as if its connection to the truck was not tight enough. I quickly informed my parents that the trailer was really rocking from side to side. They both told me that everything was fine; I probably had not payed very close attention to the trailer before. And besides, the road was bumpy. I felt a little dismayed that my parents did not trust my judgement because, you know, I was a road baby. I had spent over half of my life living in that fifth-wheel. I thought that I *should* be able to recognize what the trailer ought to look like through the back window of the pickup truck, whether the road was smooth or rough. But granted, I was only 10. So, I just dismissed my worries.

After we had safely arrived at our destination, my dad unhooked the truck. Then as he walked around the front of the fifth-wheel, he grabbed the hitch. To his surprise, it was loose! He unmounted it from the trailer and took the hitch to a welding shop. The workers informed Daddy that the hitch had never been completely welded together in the first place. Instead, the factory employees had only tacked it in four spots, and now, three of the four tacks were broken. We had towed that fifth-wheel for five years, back and forth across our nation. At any time, the hitch could have broken, and the trailer would have either smashed through the back window of the truck or crashed on the road behind us. God's hand of protection spared our lives and safeguarded our home. Truly, He made a way even when we had no idea that we needed Him to.

Although the fifth-wheel was relatively durable for full-time living, it was not outfitted for traveling 150,000 miles. It had been a faithful home on wheels for over five years. But we realized that for our lifestyle and the miles we put on our vehicles, a bus was the only reasonable option. After much prayer, research, and shopping, my parents found an entertainer coach for sale in Florida. The company that owned the bus had acres of warehouses full of busses. Shortly before Daddy flew to Florida to get our bus, a hurricane swept through that state and leveled all of the company's warehouses except for the one where our soon-to-be home was parked. Before we ever stepped foot into the black and silver coach, God was protecting it for us.

I was 10 years old in August 2004 when Daddy brought the bus to my grandparents' house in Pennsylvania. We were beyond excited to get our first tour of the inside. There were 2 living rooms, 15 bunk-beds stacked 3 high, a half bath, and a kitchenette. Although the floor plan was intriguing, it was not suitable to accommodate a family of four living in it full-time. Besides, the company that previously owned the bus had leased it out to secular bands so there was evidence of drugs and such. The interior was well-worn and stunk like cigarette smoke. We began the gutting process right away, tearing out walls, trim, beds, couches, lighting, vinyl...all the way down to the raw plywood and metal. You should have seen the burn pile at the back of my grandparents' property!

Anyways, we quickly ended up with the empty shell of a bus that was far from homey. But after a lot of bleach, Kilz sealer paint, and prayer, the interior was clean, and it smelled good too. The Lord had made a way for us to buy this new home, and my parents trusted that He would help them redesign and rebuild the inside to fit our purpose.

The goal was to make the best use of all 382 square feet. There would be three bedrooms, a bathroom, a kitchen, and a living-dining room area. Somehow, we also needed to fit a washer, a dryer, a piano, and other essentials! The rebuilding process began once we got back to California. But it was a long time coming. In fact, there are still a few uncompleted projects.

When the process first started, Daddy and Momma used masking tape on the bus floor to display the new layout. For a little while, a lime-green shop light was our only source of light in the back bedrooms. Indoor-outdoor carpet in the living room felt a little rough on the knees, but it was better than getting splinters from the plywood floors. A utility sink, microwave, and electric skillet were the appliances in our make-shift kitchen. Old, mix-match sheets doubled as curtains. The white, plastic lawn chair screwed to the floor for a passenger seat definitely served as a fashion statement. Okay, so the interior was far from attractive, but it was livable. We were roughin' it and lovin' it.

Now, almost fourteen years later, the black bus is home sweet home. The two trailers that we lived in for over eight years of traveling were a wonderful blessing of the Lord. But the bus is by far our favorite. We are so accustomed to "bus life" now that any other housing option feels abnormal. By the way, there are no more white lawn chairs, plastic sinks, scratchy carpet, or splintery wood. Each room has its own light fixtures and switches. The washer and dryer under our kitchen counter come in handy for laundry days while the oven and stove give us an excuse to make a home-cooked meal. Even the piano found a strategic location, hidden inside our kitchen table. Customizing a home on wheels has been a fascinating journey as we have watched God make a way at every stage.

Thinking back over the years of being on the road, I am amazed at how God's protection and provision are so evident. It is hard to choose which memories to share. By the grace of God, we have barely skirted danger, probably far more than we will ever know. But here are a few of those miracle moments. We left the East Coast headed for Indiana the night prior to the 9/11 terrorist attack. As we continued traveling west the morning of September 11, we were only a few short miles from the airplane that crashed in Pennsylvania. The weekend before hurricane Sandy struck New York, we were ministering at a church there, just a few blocks outside the mandatory evacuation zone. By the Sunday evening service, public transportation had already shut down in preparation for the storm, and we headed west across the local bridges only a few hours before they closed. In January 2018, our original plans were to leave Tennessee on Friday and travel west on Interstate 40. But instead, my dad chose to leave Thursday and drive south through Alabama. When the winter storm dumped inches of snow in Tennessee on Friday morning and caused a 40-car pile-up on I-40, we realized that God had made a way for us to escape disaster.

Time and again, the Way Maker has also provided financially in the midst of overwhelming circumstances. When the vehicle payments, college loans, or unanticipated bills felt impossible to manage, God moved through avenues that we never expected. Like the much needed $1,000 deposit that mysteriously appeared in our bank account or the church offerings that were miraculously beyond normal. Purchasing the white Ford F-550 we used for towing our fifth-wheel was another experience of divine provision.

It was the spring of 1999, and we had just left the car dealer. The new truck that my parents prayerfully decided to buy was the vehicle we needed for towing our fifth-wheel all across the United States. However, it was a large truck and consequently, a big investment. As my dad was driving, he began to second-guess his leap of faith. The monthly payments would be $649. There was no guaranteed work schedule, weekly salary, or backup savings account. So far, our entire journey of full-time evangelism required us to trust God for our needs. But now more than ever, faith was necessary.

A few moments later the phone unexpectedly rang. Of course, hands-free devices were not required for drivers…maybe not even existent back then! Anyways, when my dad answered, the man who was calling explained that he and his wife felt like the Lord wanted them to make our truck payment. God had stepped on the scene much quicker than my parents anticipated and with an unforeseen solution. That first month, the couple sent a $700 check which they said was to cover our payment as well as the vehicle insurance. And for the next two years, they gave us $700 *every* month to pay for our truck. The whole situation was nothing short of a miracle. What seemed like a financial barrier to us was no setback for God. He made a way through it.

On another occasion, we had plenty of bills to

go around but not enough finances. Our need was over $800, and there did not appear to be an easy fix to the problem. A dear prayer warrior called my dad to ask how he was doing. Let me make this clear, Dad does not speak to anyone about his financial situation, whether good or bad. So in response, Daddy replied that he was doing well. As she got more specific in her questioning and asked about our finances, he just affirmed that the Lord is faithful. Not willing to keep up this beat-around-the-bush stuff with my dad, the precious saint said, "God gave me a dream last night and told me you are out of money. How much do you need?" My dad was shocked. He was definitely not going to answer that last question. Instead, through the tears, he assured her that if God would tell her that we needed money, He could also tell her the right amount. She hung up the phone and sent a check for enough money to pay our bills. Through this experience and countless others, God has proven that His timing is perfect and that His solutions are beyond our finite thinking.

Now that I am older and more aware of adult-life's demands, I will admit, trusting God's timing can be difficult. I have some type of internal drive to fix things as soon as possible. If there is a problem, I will try my hardest to reason why it exists and how I can solve it. When an issue arises,

I want to know right away how the need will be met, where the money will come from, and so on. But this is where living by faith is key (2 Corinthians 5:7). Just imagine trying to run a marathon wearing baseball cleats or high heels. You would likely be unsuccessful because you do not have the right equipment. The race requires running shoes. In the same way, when we try to live only by what we can see, we will fail. This journey requires faith. From the very first time I heard these song lyrics, they hit home for me…*We will never get to walk this road by sight. Only faith will lead you through the night.* The truth of the matter is I cannot figure out or fix life's problems, and neither can you. Sight will not cut it. Instead, we need to solidify our faith in the Miracle Worker.

Maybe you are facing a mountain that looks insurmountable. The night seems terribly dark, and the burden feels bigger than you can handle. You have started believing that surely this is the trial that will take you out. Probably, we have all been there at one time or another. We try to rationalize different options and come up with solutions for God to use…as if He needs our strategies to solve the problem. When ultimately, our worrying and analyzing keep us from placing the dilemma in the Master's hands and truly believing that He will bring us through. In those rough spots on the journey when the enemy is trying to beat you down, do not give in to despair. Be your own encourager (1 Samuel 30:6). As my pastor would say, sometimes you just have to "preach to yourself." Remind yourself: *God is able. He has never failed me, and He sure is not planning to start now. This may appear hopeless, but "with God nothing shall be impossible"* (Luke 1:37, KJV). No matter what the circumstances look like at the moment, keep trusting God. I promise you, He will always make a way.

The Journey
of a
Lifetime

Chapter 3

Life on the Road

Ready or not, here I come! It was David's turn to hide, and I had just finished counting to 20 in the bus living room. While dad was driving us down the highway, we were occupying ourselves with a game of hide-n-seek.

According to our version of hide-n-seek, none of the lights could be on in the bedrooms of the bus since that was where the hiding took place. The entire center section of our coach has no windows, so it is extremely dark when we turn off those light switches. But that worked perfectly for the game. Then, whoever was the seeker had to count in the front of the bus where the lights were on and the sun was shining. This rule made the bedroom area seem even darker to the person who had just spent 20 seconds looking around the brightly lit front room.

We did everything we could think of to make hide-n-seek as challenging as it could be in 180 square feet of bedroom space. I will note that before we had the bus, my brother and I loved playing hide-n-seek in the blue and white Chevy Suburban as we traveled down the interstate. So considering the confined area we used to frolic in, hiding in the bedrooms of our coach was not that bad after all.

Now that you have an idea of hide-n-seek rules for playing in a bus, back to the story. On this particular day, we had been playing hide-n-seek for a little while. As a result, good hiding spots were getting slim, but my brother got creative. Between his bedroom and the hallway there was a temporary curtain in place of doors. When the curtain was open, the double-layer fabric bunched together against his closet. Since the fabric layers were not attached at the bottom, David separated the two sheets of material and slipped himself between them. Then when he stood erect amidst the bunched-up curtain, he was completely disguised.

I will interject a fun fact here. It is very easy to scare my mom…and really amusing too. For whatever reason, when I went to look for David, my mom walked through the hallway to her bedroom. She was clueless to my brother's inventive hiding spot, so as she passed by the curtain, it suddenly made a strange noise and started closing in around her. My brother was bear-hugging Momma through the curtain! Of course, she screamed, and then we all laughed at David's quick-witted scheme. Meanwhile, dad was still up front in the driver's seat, transporting us to the next destination. There were probably many miles to cover before we arrived at the church parking lot, and hide-n-seek helped pass the time. It was another normal travel day.

I am just an ordinary girl with a little home on wheels, a passion to make a difference, and a great big God. However, since nearly my entire journey has been characterized with traveling full-time as an evangelist's daughter, my life may seem unusual. There are many unpredictable factors of life on the road. Often, you really never know what might happen next. Even the things that are routine to me are foreign to most people. The funny moments and unique experiences are frequent...and I like it that way. Mealtimes, church services, and everyday activities vary from place to place. Yet something about this diversity is comforting. Come with me through this chapter, and I will share a few stories.

First let me warn you, I usually live in a different town every week, or I may even move after a day or two. Some mornings I awake to the challenge of recalling which state I am in and where our bus is parked. Believe me, the neighborhoods where we stay are not always the most inviting or the safest areas, which I guess is why they need churches. A bullet hole in the church siding, a drug bust across the street, a chain-link fence and pad-locked gate enclosing the church property, a nearby gunshot every now and then, or the aroma of a local meth lab...yes, these descriptions are all true. It definitely makes my journey interesting. Welcome to life on the road!

Starting school at three years old? I am not sure what I was thinking. If only I had known that I would be doing schoolwork or college assignments for the next 20 years! Regardless, my mom granted my wish. Of course, public and private school were not options because our residency changed nonstop. Homeschooling was the only reasonable choice. Since Momma was a California credentialed teacher, she became my tutor from pre-K through high school. Sometimes the bedroom, the kitchen area, the living room, or the backseat of a vehicle served as our classroom. I even did my elementary schoolwork in college classes and at campus libraries while Mom and Dad were earning their graduate degrees. Throughout my years of homeschooling, Daddy liked to claim the title of "Principal." But rather than keeping his two students in line, he would enter the "classroom" to interrupt school with tickling, wrestling, or chattering. Then the poor teacher had to get us back on track once Mr. Principal left the room! Granted, my schooldays looked nothing like the average student's classroom routine. Since our travels made regular school impossible, we adjusted to mobile education. That was just part of life on the road.

When a trailer or bus is home to four people, there is not space for much else besides the necessities. As a result, we only had one pet and not for long. Here is what happened. David and I were youngsters exploring a church yard in Missouri when we discovered a caterpillar. To our delight, Momma let us keep it in a mason jar with some foliage. We could peer through the glass walls of its home to watch our pet crawl around and munch its leaves. After a week or more, the caterpillar hung upside-down from the inside of the jar's lid. For several days, it did not eat or explore; it just dangled there. The vibrant yellow, black, and white stripes that once made an attractive design on the caterpillar's body started getting a green tinge. We were very worried that our little pet was dying.

Then one day, something strange occurred. The caterpillar converted into a bright green cocoon with shiny gold spots. As time passed, the cocoon became a clear shell, and we could see wings through the protective casing. We were thrilled when the cocoon cracked open to reveal a beautiful orange and black monarch butterfly! Now we had a new pet who did not have to live in the jar. It would land on our hands and stick out its long tongue to drink juice from a piece of watermelon. Sometimes, the butterfly sat on our textbooks or even on us while we were doing schoolwork. But after a few days of our pet flying around inside the bus, we decided to let it go free.

We were in Arkansas when Daddy carried the butterfly outside to the edge of a field. Instead of immediately flying away to freedom, our pet stayed on Dad's hand. Finally, after my dad walked about a block, the monarch fluttered away into the bright afternoon sky. Just like our pet butterfly seemed to discover, when all you know is life on the road, it is hard to imagine anything better!

Being somewhere different every week makes for an extremely fluctuating schedule. Meal plans vary drastically from church to church. Sometimes we know ahead of time what the eating arrangements will be, and other times, we are clueless until the last minute. But one thing I have learned is that life never gets boring.

Our bus was parked by the church where our family was holding a weekend revival. Saturday morning around 9:00, the pastor unexpectedly knocked on the bus door. I was sitting at our kitchen table working on a sewing project, but still wearing my nightgown. And my brother was still lying in his bunk. We were definitely not prepared for visitors. As my dad opened the door, the pastor's wife hollered from across the parking lot, "I'm hungry! Are you ready to get a hamburger?" Clad in pajamas and still trying to completely wake up, *ready* was certainly not the term to describe us kids. Furthermore, I do like a hamburger every now and then...but for breakfast? Not my cup of tea. Regardless, we scrambled around like a befuddled swarm of bees for the next few minutes to pull ourselves together. Then we piled in the truck and headed to Denny's, trying to act like everything was normal. And in a way, it was normal because life on the road is filled with last minute experiences.

Since we are constantly on the go, we do not have connections with a specific doctor or hospital for medical emergencies. As a result, I have found that super glue works wonders. Let me explain. My family and I were visiting some friends who live out in the country. We had just finished dinner when the catastrophe occurred. Momma was washing the dishes, and I was rinsing them. As she cleaned the inside of a cup, its thin glass shattered in her hands. Instantly, blood started gushing from her right hand into the sink full of soapy water. I had never seen blood literally squirt out of a wound like that. I am no doctor, but I could sense it was bad.

Despite her attempts to reduce the blood

flow with pressure, she kept bleeding through the wads of paper towels I gave her. When she briefly lifted the paper towels to show me the damage, I could tell there needed to be some stitching involved. In fact, I could see the end of a severed vein poking out from one of the gashes, which explained the excessive blood flow. We needed to do something quick, but there was no emergency room around. And besides, my mom would not have agreed to go even if the hospital was an option.

Although I had glued a few minor cuts before, this injury would be challenging. However, I was willing to give it my best shot. After a hasty discussion with my dad, the decision was made that I would drive Momma the few miles back to the bus where I could sterilize and glue her wounds. So we grabbed a stack of paper towels and headed out.

As I was driving, Momma and I were praying for the bleeding to slow down. I knew if her injury was still squirting blood when we arrived at the bus, then the glue would not seal the cuts. My other predicament was that several months before, I had fainted after seeing just a photo of an injury. Now, I was the designated "nurse" to glue Momma's hand back together; I could not afford to pass out! When we unwrapped the paper towels to clean the lacerations, the bleeding had nearly stopped. It was definitely a divine intervention. I could now see 2 one-inch cuts on the back of Mom's hand that needed to be fixed.

After applying a thick layer of super glue to the first cut, I did my best to push the visible end of the severed vein back under the skin before gluing the second gash. Since the cuts were at her knuckles, we used a spatula as a splint to keep her hand straight. For about a month, I helped Momma doctor her lacerations, which healed nicely with no infections. Often, you never know what life on the road will throw at you, so you just creatively deal with the bumps and bruises as they come.

Spending hours on the road every week, David and I came up with interesting ways to occupy ourselves. As kids, we used to pack several bags and containers full of toys to bring with us in the truck. Upon arrival at our destination, our mobile playroom looked like a tornado had swept through a toy store. Because we frequently succeeded in cluttering the whole back of the car, Mom and Dad eventually limited us to one backpack each. The new rule might work fine for David, but one backpack was just not big enough to hold all my treasures that I *needed* with me for the travel days. Baby doll clothes and cotton-stuffed bunny rabbits take up a lot more room than Hot Wheels and plastic army men. So I decided to convince my brother that since he did not need all his backpack space, he could stow some of my stuff in there too. I am not sure why, but he consented. Even though I only carried one backpack to the truck, I had all the belongings I needed for life on the road, thanks to my brother's innocent generosity.

Now that I am older, my role on travel days has changed. Instead of playing with toys and taking naps, I help keep the bus driver – my dad – supplied with snacks, coffee, stories, and southern gospel music. Sometimes we do cross-country trips in the bus that are over twenty hours of non-stop driving. During these long hauls, I stay up with Dad to keep him awake as he drives through the night.

Our record mad dash across America was a whirlwind trip in the faithful, white pickup. With the four of us taking turns driving three to five hours each, we went from California to Pennsylvania in about forty-one hours. After the scheduled youth retreat in Pennsylvania, we spent a day in New Jersey with relatives before heading out again. Then we had a week-long revival in Alabama, followed by Sunday services in Oklahoma. By the time we circled back to California, the odometer was nearly smoking from that three-week adventure. Of course, we gave it a slight rest before leaving with bus and truck for Missouri, less than two weeks later. A lot of miles, a lot of memories…life on the road.

A benefit of traveling across America is eating at some amazing restaurants. So, I thought I would give you a quick food tour of a few favorites. This excursion is not limited to one city; it stretches from sea to shining sea. No pictures or samples…just use your imagination and try not to drool too much!

The first stop has to be *Billy Gail's* for breakfast to enjoy a pancake larger than your 12-inch plate. Top it off with a carrot cake doughnut at *The Doughnut Plant* or a warm cinnamon raisin bagel smeared with cream cheese at *Bagels 4 U*. Then, order a slice of cheese pie (pizza) from *L & B Spumoni Gardens*, followed by a freshly filled cannoli from *Bovella's Pastry Shoppe*. Grab a loaf of chocolate chip raisin bread in the *Boudin Sourdough Factory* and try a piece of the Italian braided loaf in *Cuccio's Bakery*. When you visit *Biscuit Love*, make sure you have a buttermilk biscuit with sausage gravy and a sweet biscuit with jelly. Catch a hot roll at *Lambert's Cafe*, but do not forget to drizzle it with sorghum molasses. You have to try *Luis Jr's* salsa and hand-rolled tortillas. To conclude the tour, run by *Coffee Call* for fluffy beignets right out of the deep fryer and dusted with powdered sugar. I am sorry if I have made you too hungry. But if you ever happen upon any of these spots, think of me while you are enjoying the unique tastes of life on the road.

Just like there are new foods to experience at each café, restaurant, and bakery across our nation, traveling brings us to churches all over America that are very diverse in flavor. And believe me, some of the services have been fascinating, to say the least. It was the first day of revival. Before the Sunday morning service, the pastor set up his own video camera on a large tripod and asked my dad to video him while he took care of some church business. We were sitting about the third row back, so the pastor placed the tripod in the center aisle beside my dad's chair.

Once the congregational singing was over, the pastor stepped to the pulpit and nodded for my dad to start videoing. What happened after that nod was nearly unbelievable. "Sunday school superintendent, you are relieved of your duties. Women's ministry director, you are relieved of your duties. Secretary, you are relieved of your duties..." The list went on and on until the only people who still held leadership positions in the church were the pastor himself and the associate pastor. Meanwhile, here sits the evangelist in a center-aisle seat catching the candid moment on film. Awkward! It appeared that my dad was in cahoots with the pastor's plot, when in fact, Daddy had no clue that the pastor was going to fire his entire staff as a grand introduction to revival. Talk about a hindrance! How would the services turn out? Ironically, the revival proceeded as usual, and all the laid-off church staff attended. These types of crazy experiences make life on the road a little extra entertaining.

It is hard to know where to begin talking about life on the road...or where to end. The unique experiences are innumerable, and the good far outweighs the bad. Fast-pace schedules, last-minute adventures, creative solutions, amusing situations, and enjoyable opportunities keep life exciting. Even the everyday moments are never dull. Of course, the journey gets challenging at times, but never boring.

Although my lifestyle is obviously not the societal norm, I love being an evangelist girl. I believe that when God calls, He gives you a passion for every aspect of His will. Ultimately, when a bus, a highway, and a new town feel like home, life on the road is branded in your heart.

The Journey of a Lifetime

Chapter 4

Truth Is Marching On

Come with me on a drive down California's Interstate 5. This four-lane highway cuts through the vibrant green foothills of the Coastal Range. Scattered clusters of yellow wildflowers add a splash of color to the lush countryside. Rusty barbwire fences trail along the edges of the uneven fields and draw crooked lines across the distant, rolling meadows. There are cows grazing on a few of the grassy knolls, while other hillsides are covered with row after row of fruit or nut trees. Whether the sun is shining or the sky is overcast, the view is usually pleasant along this thoroughfare.

However, there are some sections of I-5 that give a depressing view of deserted orchards where thousands of trees were once decorated with delicate blossoms, green leaves, and sweet fruit. But now, all that remain are miles of wilting orchards and already lifeless trees. Perhaps the government withheld water from the farmers, which happens often in this area. Or maybe the growers encountered financial trouble or simply decided to move on with a different occupation. Regardless of the cause, those stretches of land are a gloomy picture of the past...a harsh reminder that vibrant life has turned into desolation.

Sometimes in this troubled world we begin to feel like we live amid an old, desolate orchard. So many individuals along our journey are desperately void of the life of Christ. Death, depravity, and destruction seem to reign all around us. Even people who once maintained a strong relationship with God are no longer interested in living by His Word or experiencing His glory (2 Thessalonians 2:3). In a sense, it seems that "truth is fallen in the street" (Isaiah 59:14). Traveling nationwide to minister in all types of locations, I can attest that many people have rejected righteousness. There are innumerable landmarks of where spiritual orchards have been abandoned, and the ruins left behind are heart wrenching. Clearly, the last days are upon us.

But even amidst a desolate society, we do not have to settle with the status quo. In fact, we cannot afford to give up now. God is still reaching, saving, calling, and reviving. Consequently, there is a work for each one of us to do. I am encouraged by the Master's promise to pour out His Spirit in the last days (Acts 2:17). In over twenty-two years of being on the road, we have witnessed this promise in action. Countless people are hungry for the life of Christ to grow in their hearts. They long for a change. And I have watched God meet them in the middle of this broken world. Take heart! Truth is marching on.

A story, a testimony, an encounter with God…a milestone on someone's journey. These are the experiences that keep us on the road. These are the moments that inspire us to continue praying, singing, preaching, sharing, and loving. These are the memories that build our faith. Sometimes, we find out right away what the Lord has done in lives. And sometimes, years eventually reveal the Kingdom work that has been accomplished. Perhaps, there are other accounts we will never know about until the other side of our finish line. Nevertheless, since truth is marching on, so will we, as messengers of the gospel.

Daniel did not normally attend church at all. He was just visiting one of our revival services. But when my dad closed his sermon and gave an altar call, Daniel responded. Tears puddled on the wooden altar as the broken young man asked Jesus to be his personal Savior. Being the last one to finish praying did not seem to bother him. He got up from the altar a different person. The following night, he came back to church and shared a story with my dad. Some of Daniel's buddies had asked him to come party with them that night after work, but he had turned down their invitation. Daniel told them that he was going to revival instead. At the end of his story, Daniel handed my dad $20. He sincerely explained that this was the money he would normally spend on alcohol at a drinking party with friends from his old lifestyle. God had redeemed this young man from sin's bondage and changed his heart, giving him a compelling desire to live for Christ (Ezekiel 36:26).

When one pastor gave his congregation the opportunity to share testimonies, a young convert eagerly stood to her feet. She testified that she had given her heart to the Lord during our revival the previous year, excitedly affirming, "And I'm still here!" Next, she explained that she was having trouble with frequent back pain. However, earlier that day, she noticed that her back was not hurting anymore. It appeared that the Lord had healed her. But just to be sure of her healing, the young lady performed a little experiment at her house. She picked up her two-year-old daughter Lindsey…there was no pain. So, she put Lindsey down and picked her up again…still no pain. After repeating this exercise several times with no back pain, she concluded that, indeed, the Lord had healed her back! There had been no special prayer line for healing during the revival. Just precious services graced with God's presence, providing opportunity for the Master to meet individual needs that we did not even know about (Matthew 6:8).

About halfway through revival in another town, a man who had never been to the church before attended one of our evening services. He was lost but searching for truth. At the conclusion of my dad's sermon, the man literally ran to the altar where he found the Savior. His life was transformed. After faithfully attending the church for a few months, he became an usher and joined the choir. A couple years later, he married the pastor's daughter. Every time we return for revival, we get to see the man who is now a dedicated follower of Christ. It is hard to even imagine the person he once was when he first stepped into the church. God made a completely new man from this empty life (2 Corinthians 5:17).

A big white tent, sawdust on the ground, neighbors calling the police…we were having a full-on, old-fashioned camp meeting. The Lord was moving in a powerful way during that outdoor revival. On the last night, a church member, Lisa, brought her unsaved aunt who had just been diagnosed with a brain tumor the size of a plum. Towards the end of the service, Lisa, asked my parents to pray for her aunt's healing. Mom and Dad anointed Lisa's aunt with oil and prayed, but nothing spectacular seemed to happen. Several weeks later, we received a letter from Lisa. She explained that her aunt had gone to the hospital for surgery to remove the brain tumor. In preparation for surgery, the doctor shaved the aunt's head and performed one final scan to see the exact location of the tumor. When the surgeon checked the scan results, there was no brain tumor! The Great Physician had miraculously removed the cancer (1 Peter 2:24).

It was Father's Day, and my dad was the Sunday morning speaker. He preached fervently about staying on-guard against the devil's devices to infiltrate our lives. Also, he specifically encouraged men to be the godly heads of their families and shield their homes from the sin that would try to intrude. At the close of his sermon, Daddy asked for the husbands and fathers who were willing to be the spiritual protectors of their homes to come forward and bring their families. The altar area filled as one man after another brought his family to the front of the sanctuary. From the platform where I played the piano and sang, I watched in amazement at the response. Even though we had annually ministered at this church for several years in a row, I had never seen some of these men shed a tear or even come to an altar. But as my dad made his way through the crowded altar area to pray with each family, men were crying and praying. It seemed that a determination gripped their hearts to decide, "As for me and my house, we will serve the Lord" (Joshua 24:15). Truly, the Holy Spirit was present in such a wonderful way, drawing fathers to be men of God.

Selena was a young woman with a Catholic background who had just given her heart to the Lord and started attending the church where our family was ministering. She and her boyfriend came faithfully to the revival services and brought their little daughter with them. During our revival, Selena desperately wanted to be filled with the Holy Spirit. So she would pray at the altar nightly, seeking more of God. One evening after church, we went to eat at a restaurant with the pastor and about twenty-five church people. Among the group of believers were Selena and her boyfriend. At the table, Selena started talking with my mom about how much she wanted to experience the baptism of the Holy Spirit, and she did not know why she could not seem to get through. Then she genuinely asked, "Do you think it is because my boyfriend and I are not married, but we are living together?" The question was definitely unanticipated, and my mom replied with a gentle "Maybe." Before we left the restaurant, Selena and her boyfriend decided to get married...the very next night!

We had the privilege of helping the pastor and church people pull together a wedding in less than twenty-four hours. In accordance with the young couple's wishes, the precious wedding ceremony was immediately followed by revival service. After church, there was a beautiful reception for the new bride and groom. This schedule obligated the young couple's unsaved family to be in revival. The night after the wedding, God granted Selena's desire and filled her in a glorious way. We had not told Selena that her lifestyle was immoral. Jesus had cleansed her heart and begun the lifelong process of sanctification. Selena recognized that being a Christian meant living differently from the world (Ephesians 5:8). And she was eager to do what was pleasing to her Savior.

Years before, Jim had known Christ but walked away. During our revival in his town, Jim stopped by our bus one day to give a financial gift to my dad. Using the simple words "Come on home," Daddy encouraged Jim to get back in church and rededicate his life to God. When we returned to that area for revival the following year, Jim and his wife were both serving the Lord and faithfully attending church. Jim shared with my dad that those words "Come on home" kept ringing in his heart until he could not stay away any longer. He decided to come back home to the Father's house and surrender his life to the Savior Who was waiting to forgive and restore (Jeremiah 3:22).

One evening in revival, a lady joyfully testified that God had delivered her from cigarettes the night before. And she had gone all day without smoking! For the rest of the revival, every night after service she would inform my dad how many days it had been since she smoked a cigarette. Even when we ministered at her church the next year, she reported how many months she had been free from the addiction. This sweet lady lived in a home where other people smoked, so the looming temptation was a consistent factor. Nevertheless, the Lord empowered her to resist temptation and live victorious. She experienced true liberty in Christ (Luke 4:18).

I was just a little girl during this tent revival, but I can still remember the two sisters who had recently accepted Christ and received deliverance from major involvement with witchcraft. God had broken the chains of sin from their lives. Now these two ladies were faithful to revival and hungry for truth. Towards the beginning of the week, they told the pastor that they had some things from their former lifestyle that they wanted to get rid of. So, the pastor announced to the congregation that on

Friday evening after service, we would have a barrel burning.

Immediately following the last night of revival, we all gathered around the metal burn barrel outside the tent. Those two ladies brought their witchcraft books, a tiny altar, tarot cards, crystal balls, and charms and began throwing the items into the fire. Then other church people disposed of things such as evil video games, alcohol bottles, and a bag of what one girl called her "attitude clothes." No one told the people what to burn. They began recognizing on their own the things in their lives that did not reflect Jesus. Standing under the starlit sky, watching the fire burn a barrel full of remnants from their sinful past, the believers testified of the work that God had done in their hearts. Then together we sang and worshipped God for the difference He made in their lives (Acts 19:19).

These stories are only a few examples of the countless times we have seen evidence that truth is marching on. God still changes lives. And the transformations are beautiful. Salvation, healing, deliverance, restoration, hope…each one is a unique reflection of the promise in John 8:32, "And ye shall know the truth, and the truth shall make you free." This is why we hitch the truck to the back of the bus every week and hit the road. This is why we keep pressing forward even when our bodies are tired. This is why we stay on the evangelistic field in spite of the hard times. Ultimately, life-changing truth is what compels us to sing another song, preach another sermon, say another prayer, hug another neck, drive another mile.

The past 22 years of full-time ministry have been an amazing journey. Just to know you have helped inspire someone to keep walking with the Lord, it is beyond rewarding. When the mercy of God is extended to society's outcast, or a broken relationship is mended; when the Holy Spirit falls in one of those throw-down services where people are crying, running, and shouting; when a revival continues for two, three, or four weeks because the Lord is moving in a powerful way; even when someone comes to church disheartened and weary but leaves encouraged and determined to hang in there…we are reminded that truth is marching on.

The Journey
of a
Lifetime

Chapter 5

Reaching for Another Generation

∾◦⟊◦∾

No one enjoys a stroll down memory lane like I do. Since my memories are sprinkled all across America, the stroll might be a long haul for some people. Nevertheless, I love thinking about the good ole days, revisiting the places where I first made the memories, and reliving special traditions with family or friends. I have found that the years swiftly pile up behind us as time continues adding to our individual stories. Things change. Friendships come and go. Doors open and close. Extraordinary moments fade into the mists of yesterday. Sometimes it feels like the pages of life turn faster than I can finish reading all the lines. The closing punctuation mark of one chapter is quickly followed by the capital letter at the beginning of the next.

Even though I still feel like a kid at heart, just a glance over my shoulder at the miles I have traveled makes me think otherwise. In a way, I feel like high school was only yesterday, but I am already a teacher myself. When college students look young to me, I really recognize that my days as a care-free youngster are long gone. Occasionally, it still seems weird to be the grown-up in a group of adolescents. Yet regardless of my wishes to pause the clock, time ticks on. And with my transition to adulthood has come the fulfilling opportunity to reach behind me on the journey of life to grab the hands of the next generation.

Just like my memory lane is swiftly lengthening as the years fly by, the passing of time unfolds a life story for every individual. Our personal narratives are hurriedly written by the choices we make on a daily basis. But these stories are long remembered by the impact our choices have on the world…whether positive or negative. Ultimately, life is only a vapor (James 4:14). In light of eternity, even for teenagers, the white sand is pouring to the bottom of the hourglass of time. Nevertheless, I love the potential in young people, and I have a passion to see it channeled toward fulfilling God's destiny. Indeed, the hour is pressing. I am convinced that now is the chance to make a difference. And I want my brief journey to be characterized by reaching for another generation.

Across the nation, we are met with many

opportunities to influence young lives. The responsibility is humbling, exciting, and frightening all at the same time. A negative impact can be just as detrimental as a positive impact can be beneficial. We recognize that the decisions these adolescents make today will affect them for the rest of their fleeting journey. So regardless of the setting, our goal is the same: help young people find the Savior, encourage them to follow God's calling, inspire them to be bold and unashamed, and motivate them to touch their world for Christ.

Youth camp is no vacation spot to catch up on rest, especially when you are ministering at eight services and getting only four to five hours of sleep each night. But I absolutely love the fast-paced week. It is a highlight of my year. The kids at the youth camp are inner-city teenagers. It is hard to adequately explain what that means. But I will say this, it makes for a very entertaining experience. They are animated, loud, and enthusiastic, yet at the same time, extremely respectful and affectionate. Their humor and bluntness are constantly making us laugh while their genuine love for our family is a consistent encouragement.

The late-night Sword drills and Bible quizzes are action-packed experiences that I thoroughly enjoy emceeing. Competitive vibes are prevalent, and nerves are tense. The young people are serious about their Bible knowledge and about winning. Every year, we teach them a new theme song for the week. Of course, we play on their competitiveness by doing guys versus girls competitions or one side of the sanctuary versus the other to see which group can sing the camp song louder. Activities, meal times, sports, campfires, and group devotions are all sources of special memories.

Now I will note that I do not participate much in the sports. This is not because I do not like sports but simply because running a treadmill at the gym is pretty much the extent of my athletic ability! I am perfectly content to watch from the sidelines, cheer for all the players, snap pictures, transport water bottles, and safe-guard cell phones, sunglasses, and wallets. I will jump in the volleyball games, but not necessarily to the benefit of my team…just to have fun with the kids.

From our leisure hangouts to the unforgettable church services, the teenagers' desire for God is evident. They inspire me with their sincerity and zeal. Some of the altar times after my dad preaches have been two hours or more of God's power at work in tender hearts. As the young people sit, stand, or kneel at the front of the little meeting room to seek the Lord, I get to watch from the piano while the Holy Spirit moves. For a few of the evenings, my dad or brother will take over the piano playing partway through the altar time so I can pray with the youth. Those hours spent in the presence of the Lord have been transforming milestones on the journeys of many individuals who attend the youth camp. Just for a moment, I will take you back to a few of these life-changing experiences.

Christina was about sixteen years old when she first came to youth camp with her friends. She was a sweet girl, but very reserved. Usually, Christina came forward with the other girls during the altar times but without much emotional response or evidence that she was really praying. However, Thursday night was different. When my dad gave the altar call, Christina walked to the altar area and stood quietly with her head bowed. Tears streamed down her face leaving mascara lines as Christina surrendered to the Savior (1 John 1:9). The following excerpt from the note she wrote to our family was a wonderful explanation of how she felt about the new life she found in Christ: "I accepted God into my heart today, and it was the most beautiful experience ever. I will never forget this day."

The presence of God was new to many of the young people, and they were loving every minute of it. During the second year that we ministered at the youth camp, we had such an amazing service Wednesday night that I still have it marked on my calendar. The Holy Spirit was moving in a special way. Levi, a fourteen-year-old boy who was remarkably hungry for God, had previously told his mother that he wanted to be a preacher like Brother Mann. Now, if you have ever watched my dad preach, you know how energetic and active he is when the anointing is on him. For those of you who have never seen it, let me give you a quick mental picture. He runs across the platform, up and down the aisles, and once in a while around the sanctuary. He jumps and sometimes he even hops on one leg and kicks the other. He is not soft-spoken or reserved by any means. Rather, he is very enthusiastic about sharing the gospel with his audience.

I have seen other preachers who were animated too, but I had yet to see one who kicked his leg like Daddy…that is, until the incredible Wednesday night service of youth camp. Levi had been fervently seeking God at the altar area. Soon, the Holy Spirit overflowed in his heart, and he was praying aloud, jumping, worshipping…and yes, kicking his leg. I felt as if I was looking at a teenage version of my dad. The anointing seemed to spark the same style of reaction in both of them. From the piano, I watched through watery eyes as the Lord was equipping a young man for the ministry. Levi could not contain his excitement as he embraced us and his family. We cried tears of joy with him for what the Lord was doing in his life (Isaiah 6:8). As the years have gone by, the call of God is very evident on Levi. He has a love for God's Word, a burden for the lost, and a heart for the ministry.

During youth camp one year, a teenage girl wept and prayed for a very long time at the altar. Suddenly, she grabbed her cell phone and ran out of the small conference room. She called her father to ask his forgiveness for the hurt that stood between them (Colossians 3:13). God brought restoration to the father-daughter relationship just in time. Less than two years later, her father passed away.

There were three young people in particular who I wanted to see experience the fullness of the Holy Spirit indwelling their lives. When we left youth camp in 2015, I felt like I should do some fasting to see this desire fulfilled. So, for the next year, I fasted once a week and then went on a 6-day liquid-only fast in the spring of 2016. In comparison to some stalwarts of the faith, my fasting commitment was minor. But it was a huge deal for me.

I am going to briefly chase a rabbit trail here. Fasting is not easy. I know! You feel hungry and weak, your brain gets foggy, your stomach hurts, you have obsessive cravings, or whatever else. Believe me, it is much easier on our flesh to forgo the whole fasting concept. However, I have seen God answer many prayers that were important to me and do some amazing things as a result of fasting. If you have not fasted before, or even if it has just been a while, let me encourage you to try it sometime (Matthew 17:21). You never know what God will do!

Back to my story. I had a major request that I was desperate for God to fulfill at the 2016 youth camp, and I determined to fast and pray about it (Mark 2:20). By Thursday night of youth camp, each one of those three young people had experienced a glorious encounter with the Holy Spirit. I was thrilled to watch my prayers answered right before my eyes (Acts 2:38-39).

The entire week was monumental for me. Every meal I fasted the past year had been well worth it! Praying together with my sweet friends, crying together in God's presence, and rejoicing together about God's touch were moments that gave me a renewed determination to stay faithful to the call. Not that I ever planned on giving up, but sometimes you need mountaintop experiences on the journey to keep you going through the valleys. Over the years, youth camp has been one of those spiritual mountaintops that stirred in me an even deeper resolve than before to continue reaching for another generation.

Come along with the Mann Clan, and there is no telling where you will end up or what you will get to do; but music, ministry, or both will likely be involved. In our opinion, there is nothing like a gospel song to encourage you through the hard times, remind you to rejoice over victory, inspire you to continue striving for Heaven, or keep you awake on late-night trips! David and I love singing. Our parents do too, which can be a little scary at times. But we usually try limiting their audience to our ears only. Well, I am kind of kidding about that...at least the part about being scared of their singing. Maybe I should move on.

Anyways, my dad decided to form Revival Time Youth Choirs. During several revivals, Daddy asked all the young people in the church to come early for service. Then we would teach the kids a song for them to sing that evening. Every night of revival, we taught the young people a new choir song. Practices were always interesting. Some kids could sing, and bless their hearts, some could not. I was probably one of the "could nots" a time or two! But we had a blast singing together for the Lord. Mom directed the choir while Dad played the piano *and* directed the choir director. David sang from the drums, and I sang in the choir until my parents promoted me to the choir director position. Thinking back over the years of Revival Time Youth Choirs makes me smile inside. I have many special memories. Here are just a few.

One service in particular, the Lord started moving in a powerful way while the youth choir was singing. Mom was supposed to be directing the choir, but she took off shouting. One of our lead soloists started dancing in the Spirit too. Soon, my dad jumped up from the piano, grabbed a microphone, and preachified a little with the choir behind him. Then we sang some more. People started flooding the altars. Eventually, I took over the piano playing so Dad could go pray with the people who came forward. Some of the choir members also went down to the altars while others stayed on stage to sing with my brother and me. That evening was an amazing outpouring of God's presence, and the youth choir got to be right in the middle of the experience.

It was a Friday night of revival. Some of the congregation from another church where we had ministered the month before decided to come support the meeting. They ended up bringing a bus and over fifty people! Since the Revival Time Youth Choir members from the visiting church were among the group of visitors, my dad decided to have them sing before he preached. There were around twenty-five young people who filled the small platform. Familiar tunes of "Saved by Grace" and "I'm On the Battlefield" rang through the packed sanctuary. Those young people were fired up. They were testifying, crying, singing, and worshipping. God used that Revival Time Youth Choir to encourage a fellow congregation. It was an evening to remember as the Holy Spirit graced that sanctuary in a special way through the ministry of the youth choir.

Although a majority of our youth choirs were at churches, we did not relegate choir to revivals. Sometimes we even had Revival Time Youth Choir at camp. We ministered at an annual family camp, and the pastor asked us to teach music to the youth. Since the kids were split into three different age groups, we taught three music classes each day. My family helped a lot, but they let me kind of run the show. I guess you could say I was the spokeswoman, and they had my back. Not sure if that was a good or a bad thing, but it worked. And we had a great time.

Teaching the kindergarten and lower elementary group was pretty smooth sailing. I quickly learned to give them each a microphone, and it was instant competition…who could sing the loudest? This approach worked great for me. I just had to teach them the lyrics and the tune. No worries about prodding for enough volume. They were all trying to out-sing each other!

But those high-schoolers…they were a different story. I think some of them should have been hired as mannequins because they could sit there motionless without making a sound or a facial expression! Of course, no corporal punishment aloud. So I had to get creative. I gave them pep talks. I threatened to make them do embarrassing voice exercises. I laid down the law that whoever was not participating would have to sing into the microphone in front of the whole class. Okay, so I probably sound like the mean teacher who is ultra-strict. But I loved those kids, and I wanted them to experience the joy of ministering through song. My lectures and warnings seemed to work. And somehow, by evening service when it was time to sing, they had it together. The youth choir made me so proud when they would file up to the platform, take their positions behind the choir mics, and sing about Jesus. I realized that reaching for the next generation is not always easy, but it is well worth the effort!

Although youth camp and youth choir have been amazing opportunities to affect young lives, sometimes just being a friend to young people is the perfect chance to influence them. These connections open doors for speaking words of encouragement and giving advice. My desire is to inspire youth to fulfill God's blueprint for their lives. So I present this type of basic guidance...Do not worry about what other people think when you serve the Lord. If you are a Christian, someone along the line is going to hate you (John 15:18-19). But who cares what critics think. Focus on your relationship with Christ. Trust God with your future. The Master has your best interest in mind, and His plans for your life are amazing. Seek His will (Romans 12:2). Sell out for God, and He will orchestrate the details (Matthew 6:33). I promise you, He can pave a much better journey than you could ever imagine.

I may sound blunt. But sometimes you have to talk straight with young people. Sometimes it could be a life or death conversation. The devil is out for their souls. He will try any way he can to steal them, and he plays for keeps (John 10:10). In these last days, it is a fight to keep the youth. Yet I believe that reaching for another generation is a challenge worth facing.

Young people choose role models. They strive to be like their heroes. They pattern their lives after someone they look up to. I have learned that being in the ministry often places you in a prime position for scrutiny. Moreover, working with youth is a huge eye opener that people are constantly watching your life. Through the years, I have been shocked when I find out the minor details that young people notice about how I live. The thought that your actions could affect someone's eternity is very sobering. I would never want anything in my life to deter anyone from reaching their full potential in Christ.

There are some young people I meet who I will never get to teach a choir song to or share a piece of advice with. However, they will see my life. What will they glean from my example? Will it inspire them to whole-heartedly follow the Lord and dedicate their future to God (Numbers 32:12)? Or will their journey be characterized by times of backsliding and indifference because they saw me begrudgingly serving the Master? The responsibility of teaching by example is so important that God's Word gives this straightforward commandment: "Be thou an example of the believers, in word, in conversation, in charity, in spirit, in faith, in purity" (1 Timothy 4:12). What a commission! Wherever my journey leads, I pray that every person I encounter along the way will see Christ in me.

In reality, we are all touching the next generation. Whether you are in ministry or not, someone is watching your life. Determine to walk with Christ. Live in such a way that no one can deny your dedication to the Lord. Then make this verse your motto: "Be ye followers of me, even as I also am of Christ" (1 Corinthians 11:1). As our journey quickly fades into a memory lane behind us, we are blazing a trail for someone to follow. Each one of us has to determine the legacy we leave behind. What will young people's future look like if they follow our example, and what will be their final destination? Reaching for another generation is crucial...may our influence engrave an eternal mark for Christ.

The Journey of a Lifetime

Chapter 6

The Unexpected

The sun was just setting into a brisk autumn evening when my brother and I eagerly strapped ourselves into the two-seater rollercoaster cart. We both were bundled up in jackets, ear muffs, and gloves, so the 40-degree weather was no threat to our fun. It was our first ride on this particular rollercoaster, and a majority of the wooden track was hidden behind a mountain. Considering these factors, we had no idea what to expect until we were on the rickety, 70-mile-per-hour trip over the timber beams and metal rails. Acceleration up the initial hill was our first surprise. And then those repetitive rolling hills at the end of the track…it honestly felt like we were kangaroos! I laughed the entire ride until my stomach ached, and I was having to brush the tears from my eyes as we pulled back into the station. Of course, we quickly got back in line to ride again, but somehow, it was not as funny the second time around. The rollercoaster just did not have the same effect when we knew what was on the other side of the mountain.

In a similar way, the amazing moments of life often seem more incredible when they are a total surprise. And the challenging situations are even more brutal when we do not see them coming. Although unforeseen jolts, obstacles, hills, and turns make life's excitement and pain feel more intense, these experiences build our character. They help define our true integrity under the pressure of anger or elation. Often, our reactions to the unexpected can make or break our reputation. Yet in those trying times, be reassured that God never gives us more than we can handle with His strength (1 Corinthians 10:13). Through personal experience, I have found that the unexpected can enrich our individual stories if we will accept it as a necessary part of our journey.

My life as an evangelist's daughter can be very unpredictable...more times than not. As a result, I am definitely no stranger to the unexpected. In this chapter, I would like to share several memories of unexpected encounters. A few of which were inspirational and exciting; others were hurtful and frustrating. Some may even seem insignificant. But each of these unexpected situations were landmarks along my journey. And from each unexpected moment I learned that God sees the bigger picture. He allows us to have surprising experiences, both good and bad, for a reason...even though we may not understand His purpose at the time.

During the summer of 2012, I had an opportunity that I will never forget. First, let me briefly take you back to some surrounding circumstances that made the unexpected moment even more meaningful. My uncle was gravely ill with cancer, so my mom flew to Indiana to help care for him during the last month of his life. Meanwhile, back in California, my dad, brother, and I were trying to continue the ministry responsibilities and home duties without Momma...not an easy or enjoyable task. But we managed because we knew it was best for Mom to be with her brother. However, my eighteenth birthday fell during those weeks she was away from home. For this 17-year-old girl, that was worse than holding revivals *or* doing house work without Mom. I would have to turn 18 without my momma there to celebrate with me, and 18 is a pretty monumental birthday, at least to a teenager who is approaching that "adult" age. No birthday cake, no special meals, no family party...but that was my choice. I refused to let the day feel too festive with Momma gone.

To compensate for the circumstances, my parents surprised me with a plan to celebrate my birthday in August. I was thrilled when I found out that their gift to me was a few days staying at a campground in the lush hills of Missouri while attending a southern gospel music event. Relaxing family time in the country and listening to those good ole gospel tunes I was raised on – in my opinion, that is a top-notch eighteenth birthday celebration.

The first evening concert was outdoors, which was a great venue once it started getting dark and the air cooled down. However, we were at the amphitheater early to get a close-up seat, enduring the hot afternoon sun and the hard, plastic benches. But I did not care because an amazingly talented, world-renowned gospel artist was soon to appear. I knew his songs by heart. I could pick his distinct voice out of a crowd. I had grown up listening to his music. He and his family were at the top of my favorite gospel singers list. It was hard to believe that I would finally get to meet him and watch him sing in concert, not just on YouTube! I was ecstatic, to say the least.

As the artist stepped out on stage, anticipation rose, and his familiar voice filled the air. His untucked button-up shirt, blue jeans, and snip-toe cowboy boots added to the rustic, country feel of the concert setting. For the next two hours, uplifting music resounded through the outdoor amphitheater, packed with somewhere between 4,000 and 5,000 people. My family and I worshipped the Lord, cried, laughed, and sang along with all those inspiring songs I knew so well. Forget about the entertainment, we were havin' some church!

The musical prelude to the final song "When He Was on the Cross" was bittersweet. Yet spirits were still high as the artist eloquently sang the first verse while meandering through the aisles and greeting people in the crowd. Soon he reached the second verse...*Blood was on that scarlet robe, and it had stained crimson red. Though His eyes were on the crowd that day...* He paused mid-sentence and said, "This girl has to sing." No one knew who he was talking about. I mean, there were over 4,000 people in the amphitheater! He marched down the cement stairs and across the front of the outdoor arena towards where I was sitting on the second row. Then he continued with the song...*He looked ahead in time...* Suddenly, the artist stopped right in front of my seat, looked directly at me, and paused his singing to ask, "Do you sing? A little? Come here." At that moment, I could not wrap my mind around what was happening. Talk about the unexpected! He motioned for me to stand up, so I rose to my feet. My knees were shaking, and my heart was pounding.

As the artist climbed over the front bench to stand beside me, he continued singing...*For while He was on the cross...* Then he interjected, "I've watched you. You've sang every word tonight." He slipped his arm around my back, resting his hand on my shoulder. I returned the favor, but with a death grip on the back of his shirt.

The artist finished the verse's final line...*I was on His mind.* With a genuine smile and a kindhearted tone, he asked my name. Then he turned to his band and said, "Is this a bad key for a girl?" My thoughts were in a blur of crazy emotions. The unexpected moment was thrilling and yet terrifying at the same time. Sing? With this southern gospel star holding his microphone to my mouth? In front of a 4,000-member audience? I could have fainted from shear nerves. But the band played an intro...so what else could I do? As I started to sing the chorus, the artist blurted out, "Ok, wait! Stop. Go up to a girl key." I got to pause for a minute while the band changed keys, but soon the music was ringing through the amphitheater again, which meant I had to sing higher and louder now! Honestly, I had never sung the song before...other than when I listened to the CD at home. Believe me, there were plenty of flat notes and a few sharp ones too. Sometimes the artist told me the words as I sang; sometimes he joined in with a harmony part. But I did my best under the extreme pressure. I sang from my heart, and the Lord helped me.

After I finished singing, the artist gave me a tight hug of approval and headed back toward the stage. I sat down in astonishment. He could have chosen any other person in the massive crowd of southern gospel fans, but he picked me. The singer had no idea about my late birthday celebration or my little-girl disappointment of spending my birthday without Mom. But God knew, and He used this gospel artist to bless me in an extra special way.

That unexpected moment may seem trivial. However, for me, it was a first-hand experience that God truly cares about the little things in our lives. If He keeps track of the sparrows and counts each hair on our heads, why should we discredit His desire to be involved with our daily activities (Luke 12:5-7)? Throughout my life, I have talked to the Lord about situations that others would probably think I was crazy for praying about. But I believe that God delights in moving on behalf of His children, whether the need is great or small. God is willing to intervene if we are willing to ask. You may suppose that some things that matter to you are too insignificant for the Master. This idea is so far from the truth. When the devil can successfully convince you that your needs are too small, he can keep you from taking them to the Lord. In turn, you will try to bear your own burdens without the divine strength available to believers. Do not be afraid to talk to God about your everyday cares and minor troubles. He is concerned with each aspect of your life. Never disregard God's eagerness or ability to work out even the minor details of your journey.

Before I share one of the deepest unexpected valleys I have been through, let me take you to one more of the mountaintop experiences that made an impact on my life. It was an exciting door of ministry that the Lord opened for my brother and me. Here is a quick rundown of how we ended up in the middle of the unexpected. I had vaguely heard some information about a southern gospel music convention located in California. The group who presents the West Coast conference was singing at the large southern gospel music event in Missouri that had become our annual family getaway.

Now I will clarify, sometimes I am quite ambitious, and I like to think that it is a God-given character trait…at least I hope I always use it that way! Maybe that is something I should work on. Anyways, I was having one of my many ambitious moments, so I approached one of the singers who I knew was involved in putting on the West Coast music conference. I briefly told him about myself and my brother: that we are from California, that we sing southern gospel, and so on. When I mentioned that we were interested in getting involved with the California music event in some way, he gave me two email addresses for making contact with he and his brother about the conference. With the help of my very supportive momma, I typed up an email and sent it off. Really, I was hoping to just have the opportunity to work a product table for one of the singing groups or to help behind the scenes. And I halfway expected nothing to become of that email.

When I received a voicemail from the local event coordinator for the California music convention, I was shocked. He went on and on about how excited he and the other event managers were for young people to be singing southern gospel and for us to bring "new blood" to the convention. He said that they had visited our website, listened to samples of our CD, and were pleasantly surprised about our singing ability. Now I have not decided if that was a compliment or not. Was he saying that we did not look like we could sing, but we actually could? Not sure. But regardless, my heart was pounding. I did not exactly realize that I had signed up for this. Standing behind someone else's product table to sell CDs and t-shirts is one thing. Being the singer at a concert is something totally different. My brother and I were very accustomed to singing at church...but a music convention? We were not opposed to the idea; we just had never done that before! Since I was the one who opened my mouth in the first place, the rest of my family voted that I had to be the spokesperson for the scheduling details.

During my initial phone conversation with the event coordinator, he gave me a general schedule of events and explained our options for singing at the convention. The coordinator expressed that he really wanted us to sing on main stage in the morning matinee, but he noted that there were several reasons this would not happen. There had never been a duet on the main stage for the morning concerts, and usually groups have to be involved for several years before they get to be on the main stage. Futhermore, promoters and sponsors would likely not agree to override both of these unwritten policies for a group they had never heard of. Regardless, the event coordinator promised to be our advocate. After several weeks of sending reference letters to the event coordinator, emailing back and forth, and having phone conversations, the Mann Clan was scheduled to perform Friday and Saturday afternoon at the courtyard concerts. We were perfectly content with this decision; in fact, we were thrilled. After all, the main stage sounded frightening.

The Friday morning of the music convention finally arrived. We had barely loaded our product into the event center and begun setting up our booth when the coordinator came to greet us. While he was giving us a tour of the concert hall and backstage, he mentioned that in about fifteen minutes, we would need to be back in the stadium to sound check on main stage. Our minds were spinning. Why would there be soundcheck on main stage at 9:30 AM for the afternoon, outdoor concerts? When we asked the event coordinator to clarify, he said this soundcheck was for the performers at the morning matinee that started at 10:50 AM. We were singing on main stage in less than two hours!

David and I were already nervous enough about singing at the courtyard concerts while people were eating dinner. But the idea of singing to a group of nearly 600 people who were not preoccupied by a plate of food or a dinner-table conversation was nothing short of terrifying. Besides, who knows what big-name group could be backstage during the matinee. But what could we do? The event coordinator had put us on the schedule. So we were better off using our 10 spare minutes to plan a set list and head into the stadium than stressing about it. Our parents always engrained in us that we do not sing or minister for people, we do it all for the Lord. I agree 150%. Yet no sarcasm intended, regardless of who you are singing for, a six-foot stage, spotlights, professionals, and over 500 faces staring at you are intimidating factors. At least that is how my brother and I felt when we climbed the steps to the stage for sound check.

Soon, the morning matinee was in full swing. When our turn came to sing, the coordinator's introduction was kind, the crowd was welcoming, and the sound crew was efficient. Yet we hit the stage with our confidence in God because we knew that in ourselves, we were not qualified. After singing four songs and spending perhaps the most nerve-racking 12 minutes on a stage we had ever experienced, we climbed down the stairs and headed backstage with the realization that the Lord had enabled us to sing amidst the intense pressures. He had opened an amazing door of ministry, but He did not leave us to perform alone. God walked with us through the unexpected.

This divinely organized opportunity taught me that God will open the doors He wants me to walk through if I will determine to live His plan. And I have learned that sometimes those doors are extremely unexpected. Yet when we are caught by surprise, God sees the bigger picture, and His plan is perfect. Truly, my experience was confirmation on a personal level that God orders the steps of His children (Psalm 37:23). If we will trust God with our lives and ministries, He will open doors that are nothing short of miraculous. And then God does not stand back and watch to see if we can manage the situation on our own. Rather, He walks by our side to guide us through the open doors.

So let me encourage you to be sensitive to the Master's leading. God wants to order your steps if you will let Him. He desires to open unbelievable doors if you will remain faithful on the journey. Never let feelings of insecurity or thoughts of being unqualified keep you stagnant at the threshold. Walk resolutely through the doors He opens, and remember, He will walk with you.

Over the years, I have discovered that the unexpected is not always an exciting experience like the earlier stories I shared in this chapter. However, I do know first-hand that God always uses the unexpected as teachable moments to benefit His children in some way. With that in mind, let me share one of the hardest things I have had to face. Looking back now, our family can see years of clues, but beforehand, we were quite unaware. We gave people the benefit of the doubt.

We brushed things off. We forgave. We overlooked. Then when the storm struck, it was totally unexpected.

Our friendship had once been strong. I honestly cannot give you a specific time when things started shifting. All I can say is it just felt strange. We really did not know what or why. So we tried to ignore it. Subtle comments and unexplainable actions were things that, with the Lord's help, we disregarded.

Let me interject this. When you have traveled for 23 years, you have met people with all kinds of personalities. Some people simply do not have tact. They say what they think, how they think it. And they do not bother pondering the message that their words could convey to their listeners. When you are in ministry, you just learn to be tough. You deal with the different personality types. People say rude or degrading things, and you excuse the remarks. Quite honestly, this is the approach we took through years of awkward revivals and events with this pastor and his family. Besides, you never dream that people who have been your lifelong friends would turn on you so drastically.

I am going brag on my daddy here. He is remarkably quick to forgive. I have seen it in countless situations. Often, I cannot grasp how my dad has such genuine forgiveness so shortly after an experience. Regardless, we had many family discussions about bitterness and forgiveness. Ultimately, we all had to forgive. My dad's advice to us is always "Love people and go on." That is what we chose to do.

With God's strength, we approached this revival like everyone had a clean slate. No grudges. No bitterness. From the moment we stepped back onto the church grounds, we did our very best to act like nothing happened. We did not say anything about how we had been treated. That was the past, and it was behind us. Instead, we tried to pick up the friendships where we left off several years before. But strangely, something still did not seem right. We could sense awkward vibes, so we worked harder to make things feel normal. Surely it was just a mind game. Yet the pastor's command during the Tuesday night service suggested otherwise. We had to address the issue.

A low ceiling, dim lights, a dark-oak table and chairs, coffee-colored carpet, and the looming thought that there would be a serious discussion…in a way, the dining room itself seemed gloomy. When dinner was over, my mom and I went into the kitchen to help the pastor's wife while my dad and brother stayed at the table. As my father very calmly addressed the controversy, the result was anything but a simple resolution. I tried to continue working like nothing was happening. But I could hear that the discussion was getting heated. From the kitchen, I detected that the tension was heightening with the pastor's raising voice. Suddenly I realized that my name was being mentioned – frequently. My thoughts whirled. What did I do? How could I be the problem? Once I was finished helping in the kitchen, I quietly entered the dining room, and my momma shortly followed. It felt like I was walking into a nightmare.

Gossip, lies, conspiracy, disdain…it all came to light. We were their victims, especially me. The pastor and his wife as well as some of their parishioners had been watching me for years, scrutinizing my actions and behavior. Even during the revival services that week, I was under examination, though I had been oblivious to their scheme. As they made one false accusation after another, their circular arguments had no supporting evidence. Regardless, the pastor and his wife were utterly convinced I was a hypocrite. I could not believe what was happening…I had never stood in the middle of a personal attack like I was experiencing. The conversation seemed like an eternity. Their conclusion was they did not feel I was worthy or spiritually fit to be on their platform or to minister in music. Interestingly, they lumped my brother in the mix, and he too was unqualified for ministry in their eyes. We were astounded.

The revival was originally scheduled through Friday night. Strangely, the pastor expressed that he still wanted to finish the revival, but without my brother or me participating in ministry. My dad explained that when he preaches, his children minister in music. The Mann Clan is a family package. But the pastor would not hear of it. My father agreed to preach under the pastor's conditions that Wednesday night. However, Daddy settled that we would leave the following morning.

Looking back over the situation, I can see how God helped each one of us in a different way during the confrontation. My dad spoke with such ease and composure; it appeared he was not nervous at all. He handled himself with dignity and integrity…never raising his voice, accusing, or lashing back. It was so evident that the peace and strength of God had astoundingly swept over my daddy. Behind Dad, my brother was pacing back and forth. You could sense that he was fighting mad, but he kept his cool. My mother's wisdom was remarkable. It seemed that God was putting words in her mouth. As for me, I am not the type to stay quiet when I have an opinion – or any time for that matter. But I never spoke a word to my accusers. Despite the manifested attack of the enemy on our family, God was undoubtedly in the room.

I had barely climbed into the backseat of our truck when I started crying. Suddenly, I thought that I must be guilty of *something* if people believed so strongly that my character was tainted. I felt as if it was my fault that my dad had to endure such ruthless criticism and cancel a revival. I knew that I never wanted my actions to disgrace or hinder my dad's ministry. Yet somehow, it seemed I had overwhelmingly shamed him in the minds of this pastor and his church members. My parents and brother reassured me that nothing I did or did not do was the cause of the unexpected accusations. Rather, it was the devil trying to wreak havoc in my life and in our ministry.

We arrived back at the bus with just enough time to get ready for what would be our final revival service at this church. Oddly, I still remember my outfit! I wore a burgundy and black patterned dress with a textured burgundy sweater and a black infinity scarf. Honestly, I do not know how I was able to walk into the church that evening and face the situation again…this time knowing I was stepping into the inspection hall. I was sort of in a daze. It was one of those moments when you simply put one foot in front of another because that is all you know to do. The numb feeling of having just experienced something traumatic served as a shield against being overcome by the thoughts of current scrutiny during and after the service.

We greeted people who we knew despised me and resented our family. We prayed in the altars with them. My dad preached with exuberant fervor as usual, knowing how individuals in the audience felt about us. But the Lord faithfully strengthened us once again. We proceeded like everything was normal. Though this type of unexpected situation can be challenging to push past, we did it, at least for the night.

By the following morning, the shock factor wore off, and reality had set in. The false accusations played over in my mind. Thoughts of "Rachelle" being the hot topic of gossip and the target of irrational criticism were difficult to process. All those strange feelings and stressful days during the previous years of revivals and church events suddenly made sense. We were not imagining things at all. Those awkward, perplexing sensations were real. People *were* talking about me behind my back, creating rumors to convince each other that I was guilty of hypocrisy. And to think people had been creeping on me for years…that was the hardest element of this whole ordeal for me to grasp. I was absolutely horrified at the idea. I felt so violated. It is challenging to adequately explain the aftermath, but the situation haunted me to the point that my body was literally trembling, and my mind was overwhelmed.

We drove a few hours away to park at a church where some dear friends of ours pastored. As we backed into the driveway alongside the church, I felt like we were arriving at a safe haven. The church's Christian school had just dismissed, so the kids gathered around us with warm greetings and enthusiastic requests for us to sign their yearbooks. Clearly, the Lord was already giving us a fun, encouraging moment to counter the response our family received less than twenty-four hours prior.

That evening, the church and school had a large event planned. We all jumped in the middle of the preparation, helping in any way we could and just spending time with people who we knew genuinely loved us. From the afternoon preparation to the late-night clean-up, the evening was crammed, lively, and enjoyable. Honestly, that busy schedule was good for me because I had less time to dwell on daunting thoughts of the personal attack on my character.

After the event, our minister friend had a heart-to-heart talk with me about dealing with the situation I faced the day before, encouraging me that in these experiences, we have to just move forward. Also, he reminded me that the Bible says we will go through things, but the important factor is that we grow from the hard times. This next piece of advice that he shared stirred resolve deep in my heart: *"Don't let anyone define who you are."* It rang through my mind. It gave me grit to press beyond the assault. It inspired me to choose to be who I am in God and not cave to the descriptions of others. I clung to that advice as a motto for my life.

This unexpected valley I had to tread through was a decision ground for me. I could conceal bitterness or forgive. I could feel sorry for myself or allow the false accusations to make me tougher. I could dwell on the pain or let God renew my mind. I could believe the descriptions that my criticizers gave me or embrace my identity as a child of the King. The choices were real. The conclusions would somehow be lifechanging…no matter which option I selected.

Years ago, I determined that my journey would be characterized by my relationship with the Lord and my dedication to His plan. In order to keep moving forward in this resolution, I had to recognize that God allowed me to face the situation for a reason. With God's grace, I forgave. I put the hurt behind me and moved on. I chose to not let people define my character. I heeded my pastor's admonition to walk through an offense rather than live in it. Ultimately, the unexpected challenge that the devil meant to take me out was a refining experience to make me stronger (Job 23:10).

Unexpected moments on our journey that rouse feelings of anger, frustration, defeat, and confusion can be landmarks where we learn some of the greatest lessons. Forgiving the person or people who have treated you wrongly is foundational in overcoming a hurtful situation. Christ forgave each of us to an unimaginable degree; the least we can do is forgive others (Colossians 3:13). Really, unforgiveness does the most harm to the individual who harbors it. Bitterness will eventually control you. So determine to forgive, and God will empower you to move on.

Allow the enemy's attack to give you a greater resolve to stand for what you believe. Do not worry about what people think or say about you. Your true identity is in Christ…be a confident reflection of Him. Disregard false accusations. As a special friend and woman of God once told me: "Don't let it affect you." And then let God fight your battles. Give Him the opportunity to handle the situation (Romans 12:19). When you try to retaliate, you are only making a bigger mess and tainting your own reputation. Trust God that He has a plan for you beyond what you can see in the moment of pain. His goal is for you to be stronger after you have come through the trial.

The Journey of a Lifetime

Chapter 7

Singing or Dreaming

∞◡◜◠◞

Two kids with a big dream and an amazing God...the whole story was miraculous. We were living it, yet we still had trouble wrapping our minds around the reality of each phase that fell into place. David and I have sung together since we could barely walk onto a platform. It is our life. A shear love for listening to and singing the songs that we were raised on has kept southern gospel music flowing through our veins. And a passion to share the gospel in song has carried us on stage even in the face of fear, sickness, opposition, and trials.

One day, we started dreaming of recording our own album, yet the idea appeared very farfetched. Then, as people at churches where we ministered started asking us if we had a CD, it seemed that God was confirming our dream. But we were totally clueless to the recording process, unsure of who to ask for advice, and doubtful about our own musical or financial ability to make it happen. This was the extent of our expertise. So where should we begin? We really did not know.

There is nothing quite like a southern gospel concert in an outdoor amphitheater, nestled among Missouri's rolling hills that boast a forest of lush, green trees. The cool evening breeze is a relief from the late summer sun. And a cup of frozen lemonade is the perfect refreshing treat. Renowned Christian artists, powerful lyrics, familiar tunes, and a passionate delivery make this type of concert an experience to remember. I love such moments of inspiration…in fact, it was one of these evenings in September 2015 where our recording story began.

The voices of our favorite southern gospel family echoed through the venue. Their vocal talent and stage presence never cease to be amazing, yet they minister with such anointed fervor. This was our fourth time to be at one of their concerts. During the previous years at this particular event, we briefly met them and had short conversations together, but that was the extent of our connection. Nevertheless, my brother and I had decided to ask the father of the group for some general guidance about making a CD. Of course, since I am usually the more daring one, my brother wanted me to do the talking. But I was nervous too, I just tried not to act like it!

Though the evening sky was dark, the flood lights helped brighten the side stage where the singers were selling their product and greeting the fans. Most of the 4,000-member audience had left the venue by the time my brother and I approached the product table after the concert. I spoke with the artist who generously offered advice, suggesting that we lease 10 soundtracks and then locate a studio to record our vocals. I was surprised when he mentioned his studio among the list of several options for studios to choose from. During the course of the discussion, he even agreed to sing some background vocals for us when we eventually recorded our CD. That seemed too incredible to grasp. Then we were more amazed when at the close of our conversation he gave us his phone number and said to contact him with any questions…he wanted to help us through the process. Surely, I was dreaming.

My brother and I climbed the flights of cement steps out of the amphitheater as quickly as we could and ran almost the entire way to where our parents were waiting in the truck. We eagerly jumped in the vehicle to share our exciting news. Replaying that evening over in my mind felt like I was trying to believe a fairytale. I could not help but think that God must have a plan. And I was overwhelmed to imagine that this amazing singer was willing to be an instrument for God to use in our lives.

Let me give you a piece of inside information about the Mann Clan. We are always up for a family adventure. And most of the time, our adventures include driving! A few weeks had passed since the memorable concert where we got advice about recording. We had several days off in late September, and our favorite southern gospel family was scheduled to perform at a live recording in Tennessee. It was a Christmas-themed event, so going meant we would get to enjoy the decorations and songs of my favorite holiday…just a few months early! Also, we hoped that if we went, the opportunity would arise for us to further discuss specifics of making a CD.

By Sunday evening, we had finished our revival in Michigan. Then Monday morning, we headed south to Indiana. The more we discussed the option of leaving our bus there in Indiana and taking our truck to Tennessee, the more we all were convinced that the adventure was irresistible. Since the video recording was Tuesday evening, we needed to leave early enough on Tuesday to make the seven-hour trip. Meanwhile, we kept our plans and destination under our hat, choosing to spend a couple days completely off the grid. The final decision was made, a hotel room reserved, and we shifted into sixth gear, scrambling to pack our suitcases.

On Tuesday, at 6:00 PM, the auditorium doors opened to reveal a stage converted into a captivating holiday scene. There were rod-iron park benches, vintage street lamps, an antique carriage, white Christmas lights, evergreen trees, and gentle snow drifts. Glowing lightbulbs lined the edge of the stage at each cascading level. The deep blue and purple lighting effects and the silvery haze almost made the air feel like a frosty winter evening. It was spectacular.

For over two hours, the wonder of that silent night in Bethlehem was alive in our hearts as the performers sang familiar holiday tunes, debuted new Christmas songs, and shared Scripture verses about the birth of Jesus. Our family laughed, cried, rejoiced, and sang along. Once the production concluded and the stage lights dimmed, we had the opportunity to visit with the artist who had so generously guided our initial thoughts about cutting a record. After making plans to meet with him for a meal to talk more about recording, we headed back to the hotel…feeling like we were living a dream.

What would soon be known as our "pre-production meeting" was held at a Cheddar's restaurant. Once again, my family made me the designated spokesperson. I still have not figured out if it is good or bad to always be selected to do the talking. But regardless, that was my job for the meeting. I had a little cream tablet with gold music notes printed on the cover. There were pages filled with information that we had gathered from researching about recording and from touring a renowned Christian studio with the studio manager. In that music notebook, I had also compiled lists of questions to ask the artist during our discussion. When he arrived, he handed us the first two CDs of their brand-new release that he had just picked up from the record company on his way to lunch. That action alone was enough to make us realize that the unexplainable bond we felt with this amazing singer and his family must be a mutual connection.

During our two-hour lunch, I asked if he would consider allowing us to record at his studio, and he agreed. Since he had mentioned his studio in our original conversation about making a CD, I just assumed he let people record there. Further into the conversation, we discovered that his studio was a private one. And he normally uses it just for producing family records...we were the exception. That realization was so humbling, and it literally felt unreal. It was a dream coming true.

When he asked us the time-frame we had in mind, I said that we were thinking about waiting a year. He quickly replied that we should record by

December or January. Another remarkable aspect was that he agreed to do our recording even though he had never heard us sing a note! To top it off, the artist confirmed his commitment to sing on our CD, including a solo part. We were overwhelmed.

In fact, looking back now, I must have been in shock during that meeting. I am not sure how I was able to keep asking my questions, receive out-of-this-world answers, calmly take notes in my little tablet, and not do a Jericho run around the restaurant. The generosity of our new friend was beyond comprehension, and we were filled with gratitude. It was clearly a God-ordained moment, one of those times that is so unbelievable you are unsure how to express adequate thankfulness or love to the hero God has placed on your journey. Somehow, we all understood what our smiles, hugs, tears, and laughter communicated…this was more than a major stage of our miraculous recording story. It was the beginning of a treasured friendship that would last a lifetime.

Now that we had some of our recording arrangements established, we decided it was time to start practicing. But here is the deal; David and I were accustomed to singing with live music. In fact, we had never used a soundtrack. So we had no idea how difficult the adjustment would be. We normally played our own instruments which meant we could adjust the key, tempo, syncopation, and style to our liking – and to cover for our mess-ups. When we purchased the first couple soundtracks for our recording and tried to sing with the prerecorded band, we were shocked. It was hard…*really* hard!!! I mean, I wanted to throw in the towel right then and there. This was the first of many times throughout the next few months that I decided Rachelle was just was not cut out for recording.

Believe me, at each stage of your journey, the devil comes up with as many hinderances and excuses as possible to keep you from fulfilling God's plan. All the circumstances that had fallen into place for our recording were clear evidence of a divine purpose. But feeling inadequate, unequipped, afraid, or doubtful can quickly build a roadblock that keeps you from accomplishing what God has called you to do. Just remember, the devil is a liar, and his advice is deceptive. Resist his attempts to distract you from the goal (James 4:7). With the Lord's help, you can overcome any discouraging obstacle that the devil throws in your path.

My brother and I continued working through the songs we chose for our CD. And soon, we started feeling comfortable singing with soundtracks. Practice times were filled with figuring out the lead and harmony lines, blending our voices, and tweaking our vocal licks. Ultimately, the goal was to memorize our basic parts so our producer would just have to modify the areas that he wanted customized.

During our many hours of practicing, I would get frustrated or discouraged about my singing. David gave me countless pep talks to never say *I can't* – which is my famous line when it comes to music. Do not get me wrong, I love to sing. Yet I often struggle with hearing my part, feeling short on talent, or having the confidence to just go for it. Nevertheless, we tried to reassure each other that the target was attainable, and at each barrier, our parents would cheer us on. Even though the process was not always stress-free, we chose to keep singing and to keep dreaming.

Let me briefly insert a personal limitation I have dealt with that might help you picture the intensity of our recording preparation. Singing harmony did not come natural for me like it did for my brother. Quite honestly, singing in general is something I have had to work at, and still do! When I was younger, I could not hear a single note of harmony. However, I have prayed for the Lord's help, and my brother has worked with me for countless hours. Over the years, my ear has developed enough that I can hear and sing harmony...to an extent. Usually I still need David to at least show me a few of the harmony notes for any song I sing. Sometimes he even has to teach me my part for the entire song. But I am okay with that. In fact, I have learned that we rely more on God for tasks when we realize we are not capable of doing them on our own. If everything came easy, we would never know what it was like to watch the Lord enable us through His power. When we recognize that even our best talents fall short of perfection in light of the Master, then we are opening the door for God to enhance our abilities as the Holy Spirit equips us for the journey.

In November, I surprised my brother with tickets to a Christmas concert where our producer and his family were performing. I had to do some maneuvering to make it happen because the concert was actually part of a three-day event. Usually, tickets were only available for the entire conference. But I was able to contact the event coordinator several weeks in advance, and she graciously made an exception for my brother and me. We arrived at the resort early to be sure we got to share a slice of our favorite four-layer carrot cake from the Sweet Shop. Once the large conference room was open for the concert, we took a seat at one of the tables right near the stage.

What we did not think about was that the large speakers were directly in front of us. Now let me clarify, we like it loud. Just about any time we attend a concert, we do our best to be up close. We are front-row people. But when that holiday music started, it was ear-piercing. I quickly tore two small pieces of tissue, one for David and one for me. After wadding up the tissue fragments, we each put the impromptu ear plug in our ear that was closest to the speaker. It muffled the sound just enough to remove the sharp pain, but I promise, we could still hear every note and word absolutely fine. The problem arose when one of us would try to discreetly say something during the concert. We were cranking our necks and halfway yelling at each other to relay simple messages. I know we looked like a set of grandparents who forgot their hearing aids at home. Oh well, at least the room was dark! We just laughed at ourselves and made sure we took the tissues out during intermission.

Meanwhile, a cheerful holiday spirit flooded the atmosphere of the concert as the artists sang a dynamic compilation of Christmas songs. Then the performers concluded the second half with familiar carols and a few southern gospel hits. Amidst that evening stuffed with special memories, we set recording dates with our producer for January 12 and 13, 2016. Even though we had been singing with our soundtracks for nearly two months, it seemed unreal to actually have the recording scheduled. David and I were going to make a CD with the producer of our dreams! We could hardly believe it or contain ourselves. Shortly after the new year dawned, we would be headed to Tennessee.

Finally, that winter Tuesday morning arrived. We had practiced hours upon hours and sang through our tracks so many times that we were nearly tired of our songs before the recording even began. Yet we still did not feel prepared enough. But ready or not, we had to be in the studio at 10:00 AM. I distinctly remember the 15-minute car ride from our bus to the studio. There was a massive swarm of butterflies in my stomach. Even though our excitement level was at an all-time high, David and I were nervous out of our minds.

We were about to sing in front of our producer who was a multi-award-winning vocalist. While his musical ability is nothing short of amazing, he has such a humble spirit; so it was definitely not his personality that intimidated us. It was just the fact that he is extremely talented. In addition, our producer's personal engineer and long-time friend was going to engineer our recording. Believe me, there were plenty of factors to keep us tense. However, when we arrived, the excitement of stepping into the cozy, little studio outweighed our worries.

A worn Bible graced the small table just inside the door, and a flickering candle radiated a mild aroma. That welcoming ambiance was completed by our producer's warm greeting as the four of us entered the room. We peeled off our heavy coats and took a seat on the comfy, red couch. Just a few short months before, the idea of recording was only a wishful dream. Now, we were actually in the studio, holding our stack of soundtracks and talking with our producer. It was not a dream at all.

During the two days we spent in the studio, we laughed almost as much as we sang. Our producer and engineer had such awesome personalities, and both of those guys were like stand-up comedians. All the laughing and joking helped us be more relaxed, yet something about wearing the headphones and singing into the recording microphone was just scary! Despite our nerves, we began getting used to the process. We learned that sometimes you are "killin' it" right away, while other times you have to keep redoing the same part to "get it in the pocket." Our producer or engineer might sing a sample lick and then say, "Do me something like that." If a certain line did not sound quite right, one of the guys would tell us, "Give me one more." They tweaked some of our lead and harmony parts while adding a few fancy touches. They encouraged us to sing with heart and to let it show in our voice. They inspired our lives with their words of advice and approval.

Before we even started recording, our producer shared his goal to push David and I at our ability levels. He definitely stuck to that objective, which was very challenging at times. Nevertheless, those two days in the studio were a priceless learning experience. And over thirteen hours of studio time provided the perfect occasion to make memories out of dreams.

This part of my journey was a landmark where I recognized that God's ways are much higher than ours (Isaiah 55:9). A dream that seemed nearly unattainable came true in a more wonderful fashion than I ever envisioned. I watched how God guided my footsteps, spoke to others, and orchestrated schedules to make His will unfold.

Sometimes the Master's ideas for our lives do not appear reasonable or workable to the natural mind…it may actually feel like we are dreaming. Just remember that God's plans involve the supernatural. As you surrender your life wholly to God and commit to fulfilling the destiny that He has in store for you, your desires and dreams will align with His will. Then, He can make your dreams come true in a way you never imagined (Psalm 37:4). Do not get overwhelmed by how impossible the situation may look. Stay focused on the goal. When your dream seems inaccessible, rest assured that God sees opportunities from a different point of view. He knows how to work out details that are beyond your control, and he has your best interest in mind. I know from experience that this journey has its highs and lows. But through it all, I have determined to never stop singing or dreaming.

The Journey
of a
Lifetime

Chapter 8

His Grace Is Sufficient

At times along the journey, we have to be reminded that God knows how much we can handle, and He also knows what will reinforce our reliance on Him. Rest assured that the road of life will never become too difficult for us to bear if the Lord is our Guide. When He allows us to endure physical struggles, He has a purpose. He will give us the strength to continue even when our bodies are weak.

Let me establish that I am a firm believer in divine healing (Isaiah 53:5). I have witnessed and experienced God's healing power on numerous occasions. He is just as able to restore the physical as He can the spiritual. However, God is sovereign. He does what is best for His children. And I believe sometimes He chooses not to remove a sickness or infirmity to teach us that His grace is sufficient to sustain us through the hard times (2 Corinthians 12:9). In those moments, we learn the sweetness of depending on the Master.

As a healthy, 15-year-old girl, *physical*

disability was the farthest thing from my mind. Little did I know, that term would end up being a condition that affected me in nearly every aspect of life. I was sitting in our bus at the kitchen table, pouring over my high-school textbooks. My momma was on the couch behind me when she suddenly noticed my back looked deformed. She quickly instructed me to sit up straight. When the bulge seemed to disappear, she had me lean over the table again. With my back bent, there was definitely a visible deformity. As her last evaluation, Momma had me sit up straight a final time so she could feel my backbone. I followed her orders, not exactly sure why she was having me do calisthenics while I was trying to focus on my schoolwork.

Though I was unaware, my mom had learned how to recognize scoliosis from a friend's explanation whose daughter had recently been diagnosed. The right side of my back had a visible hump on the top portion, and my spine was an "s" shape rather than a straight line. My symptoms were undeniable. I had scoliosis.

Shortly after this incident, I can vividly remember the morning I realized that one of my hip bones was noticeably higher than the other. It was a strange feeling for a teenage girl to accept that not only was my back curved, but my physical disability also made my body structure crooked. I suffered from back pain on a daily basis. If I was sitting or standing for any time longer than 20 or 30 minutes, my back was hurting. Playing the piano, driving, and sometimes even lying down were painful. Over the next few years, there were countless chiropractor visits and back strengthening exercises.

The chiropractor confirmed that my hip bones as well as my shoulders were not level because of the scoliosis. At every appointment, I would climb onto the dull green table and lay face down, listening for the instructions: lift your right shoulder, relax, follow with your left, relax, shrug both shoulders, and so on. I could probably almost repeat the entire process. And the quiet clicking sound of his tool is etched in my mind...I heard it a lot! During each visit, my chiropractor worked on the hump in my back, attempting to lessen the drastic deformity and to reduce this source of discomfort. He also labeled the muscles along my backbone "string cheese" because they were excessively knotted and strained from their unsuccessful attempts to straighten my scoliosis.

Then around the time I started college, I began running a couple miles several times a week to help manage a circulation problem in my feet. Time passed, and I noticed that my back pain was decreasing a little. My chiropractor encouraged me to keep up my exercise routine because he could see progress in my back. However, I remember when we realized that my running and the chiropractor's adjustments had made as much improvement as possible. The remaining effects of the scoliosis would just be part of life. I had a physical disability, and I had to deal with it.

Through the years, I have learned to accept back pain as normal for me. Honestly, some days I do great while other days are very painful. Yet in either circumstance, it is not my place to feel sorry for myself or to question my Creator. People face much harder challenges than scoliosis and still live victorious, effectively fulfilling their God-ordained destiny.

More recently, I set a goal for myself. Instead of complaining when my back is hurting, I decided that I would pray for a dear friend who deals with so much more back pain than I do because she suffered a broken spine several years ago. I will admit that I have often fallen short of this aspiration. One thing I do know, however, is that when I strive to pray instead of complain, my outlook on life shifts from self-pity to optimism and resolve. Ultimately, I would love for God to restore my back. And I am so grateful for my fellow believers who I know are praying with me for my complete healing. There is no doubt in my heart that the Great Physician is more than able. But for now, I realize that God has a plan. He knows what I can handle with His strength. If I have scoliosis for the rest of my journey through this life, I believe His grace is sufficient for me.

The Journey of a Lifetime

Chapter 9

College Days

⤬⤬⤬

Here I sit on the couch with a fuzzy blanket and a laptop. I have no essays to write, no 40-page projects to work on, no lesson plans to create, no tests to study for, no textbooks to read, no vague instructions to decipher, no deadlines to worry about…yes, I am a college graduate and thrilled to be free. I can write about whatever I choose. I am not required to research the internet for peer-reviewed journal articles to support my ideas. I do not have to stay up until 3:00 AM, overloaded with assignments. Okay, so I guess you know how I feel about five and a half years of continued education. But regardless, I will share a few memories from my college days…both sweet and sour!

Many of the experiences I had in college are far from what people would consider traditional. I have nothing to say about dorm life because I never lived on campus. In fact, I did not even step foot onto the university grounds until after I started graduate school. We wanted to continue traveling and ministering as a family while I worked toward my degrees, so I attended a Christian university that offered a completely online undergraduate program.

Since my goal was to become a credentialed teacher, I chose to major in Elementary Education for my Bachelor of Science (BS). As if one degree is not sufficient for preparing someone to teach $5 + 5 = 10$, the college I attended also required teacher candidates to get a Master of Arts in Teaching (MAT). Thankfully, even my graduate program was mainly online. Also, while I was earning my MAT, I had the opportunity to work one year as an online writing tutor for the college.

In a way, life continued as normal for this evangelist girl because I still lived in the bus, traveled with my family, and stayed involved in ministry. However, I also experienced a lot of changes in ordinary life on the road. College classes, professors, coursework, and tutoring were completely foreign experiences for me. Nevertheless, looking back over my college days, I can clearly see God's hand involved with each of these new horizons.

Making a class schedule is not always the easiest task, especially when the college puts restrictions on course availability. There was one curriculum development course that my university required graduate students to take either during their student teaching or in the semester directly before their internship. I definitely did not want to deal with extra assignments while I was trying to manage the responsibilities and college work I would have during my student teaching. My other option was to take the curriculum development class in the summer of 2017 because my internship would be that fall. But here was my dilemma. On top of my tutoring job, there were two intensive courses I *had* to take in the summer, and I could not handle adding another class to that pile-up of responsibilities.

The ideal time for me to take the curriculum course was during the 2017 spring semester. So I decided to be brave when I called an academic advisor to register for my classes. Rather than asking permission, I just listed the curriculum development course along with the three other classes I was taking. I acted like that schedule was an option because I desperately needed it to be. Somehow, she was able to work around the system and register me for that class in the spring. I was delighted! This may seem like an insignificant memory from my college days, but it was a major blessing. I credit the Lord with intervening on my behalf. He knew what was best for me, so He maneuvered the details.

No, all professors are not absentminded. I

was privileged to have several amazing instructors over the past five years. However, I can speak from experience that there are some crazy professors who definitely give their occupation a bad rap. The final fall semester in my undergraduate program provided one of those dreadful experiences.

In the course I was taking, the benchmark assignment was a vague project with a million different format options. To make matters worse, the assignment was worth about one fourth of my entire class grade. So I emailed the professor to ask a question about the project I chose. She replied with a request for a phone conversation, and I agreed because I did not expect any issues to arise. Our conversation seemed to go well. I explained some specifics of my project, and she answered my questions, gave me a few guidelines, and assured me that my photo-story about differentiated instruction was exactly what she was looking for.

I worked really hard on that project, doing everything the professor told me to do and then some. The finished product made me happy, and I eagerly submitted it two weeks early. To my dismay, the professor gave me an F! I was horrified. An F? Are you kidding me? That score would drop my overall class grade a whole letter! Now let me clarify, there is nothing wrong with getting a B in a college class; that is a very good grade. But my personal goal was to graduate with a 4.0 GPA, and this crazy lady was crushing my dream only a few months away from the finish line.

When I read the professor's reasoning for the grade, I was even more upset. She subtracted points for things that she had earlier approved during our phone conversation. I tried to respectfully address the professor about the unfair grade, but she would not budge. At first, I was stressed about the situation, especially since I was having to deal with it during Christmas break. However, my momma advised me to not let the professor's actions control my thoughts and ruin our holiday fun. So I decided to dismiss the feelings of anger and frustration.

Once the course was over, I started the dreaded grade appeal. This drawn-out process was a month of frequently reexplaining the situation to college faculty, submitting additional evidence of my professor's unjust actions, and trying to reach someone who would rationally consider my issue instead of being bias toward the university employees. During that ordeal, the professor even did some unethical things to cover for the unfair grade she had given me. Regardless, I was finally able to appeal to the dean of my university's School of Education.

The Lord gave me a connection with a man who worked alongside the dean, and he graciously took my situation to heart, serving as my advocate to resolve the issue in my favor. I ended up having to write a five-page paper to explain how my project did meet all the requirements that the professor accused me of neglecting. Then, the seemingly eternal nightmare was over as quickly as it began. I received the class grade that I worked so hard to earn. The dean had chosen to override the professor's evaluation of my project. I was able to witness first-hand that God had my back…even in my college days.

It was one of those extremely busy weeks shortly after I started my tutoring job. We were on the East Coast ministering at churches and spending a little time with my mom's family. Since it was the week before midterms, I had some major assignments due. And the online graduate writing center was overloaded with tutor requests. Basically, I had no hope of any laid-back, family-centered days. Although I did try to spend as much time as I could with our relatives, I was obligated to ministry, college assignments, and work. The tutor requests were pouring in so quickly that it was difficult for me to complete my own assignments. I ended up logging about forty hours for my job. Almost every night that fateful week, I stayed up until somewhere between 2:00 and 4:00 AM, trying to finish tutor requests. Then I would fall into bed, sleep a little, and awake to another jam-packed day...convinced that if I could make it through this experience, I could survive anything!

By the last day of the week, I still had a college paper due in a few short hours. I wrote frantically during the afternoon, but I had already committed to attend a girls Bible study that evening. When I arrived back to the evangelist's quarters we were staying in, I had to finish my assignment. Now, I was literally racing the clock. I remember sitting in a straight-backed chair at the cream-colored table with Momma standing behind me. She was peering over my shoulder to proofread as I typed the paper. The atmosphere in the room that evening was tense – to say the least – because I did not dare turn in a late assignment. I tried to never give myself that option. And my parents definitely did not support a late submission. So I was writing as fast as I could.

To my relief, I turned the paper in with barely three minutes to spare! Now here is the deal...I do not recommend this chaotic timetable, but my schedule was so insane that week there was not much else I could do. In these types of stressful occasions, my parents and I would pray for the Lord to quicken my mind, to give me favor with my instructors, and to provide strength for handling the stressful workload. It may seem odd to ask God for help with college assignments, yet He says that we can bring *everything* to Him in prayer (Philippians 4:6). Nothing is too small or too great for the Master to care about. I know that God intervenes on behalf of His children. And let me tell you, I am positive that I could not have made it through my college days without His strength.

My dad was planning our ministry schedule for the fall of 2016, but there were two weeks in a row that he could not get direction for. What should we do? We had to go someplace...but where? As I began college classes for the fall semester, I was troubled to learn that one of my courses required a two-week practicum in an approved classroom. Now here I was adding an extra dilemma to our fall schedule. Back when I registered for that class, I was not aware of the field experience obligation.

My mind started reeling, trying to figure out how to make things work. Right away, I thought of a Christian academy in Tennessee that we had recently become acquainted with, and I wondered if that school might be the perfect setting for my practicum. My parents agreed to consider the option, but we only had those two open weeks in September. If the headmaster and teacher did not accept my request to complete my field experience during those two weeks, I would be in a predicament.

We stopped through Tennessee in August for me to ask about my practicum. When Momma and I went to the school, the headmaster and the third-grade teacher eagerly agreed that I could fulfill my field experience in their third-grade classroom. I was thrilled with the plans. In our conversation with the teacher, we discovered that the school was normally closed for a teacher convention during one of the weeks I needed to be there. But for some reason, the seminar was the first week of October that year. This was no coincidence. God was working out specific details of my college days that we had no idea about. He carefully organized our ministry schedule and my college program to be compatible with the school's calendar. Even before I knew that this stretch of my journey would exist, the Master already had something in the making.

Although I loved the benefits of online schooling, one of the hardest challenges was juggling college and full-time ministry. I had due dates every weekend and revival nearly every night. At the beginning of some weeks, I would look at my school schedule and think *Lord, if I do not have Your help, I realistically cannot finish everything by the due date at 11:59 PM.* I knew that there were just not enough hours in a week for me to get all my college work done. Impossible! But it was in those times of intense pressure that I truly learned to lean on God. I experienced the truth of Matthew 19:26… "With God all things are possible." If He opened doors for me to attend an online university while I was in full-time ministry, then He would empower me for the task. My responsibility was to do my best and to trust God (Ecclesiastes 9:10). Somehow, everything always got done. God never failed to pull me through.

Then in September 2016 when my university hired me as an online writing tutor for graduate students, I was adding a part-time job on top of my busy lifestyle already packed with college and ministry. There were days I was absolutely swamped with my own schoolwork as well as with other students' essays to proofread. Sometimes I felt that if I took off running, maybe I could outrun the pressure of college assignments, tutor requests, and deadlines.

On a side note…I did run hundreds of miles during my college days, but I *never* outran the stress of a crammed schedule! There were always more projects and papers to complete. If I had given my mom a quarter for every time I said "I quit," she would be a wealthy woman today. I am not one-hundred percent sure what I even meant by that frequent declaration "I quit"…except that I did not think I could survive the rest of the schoolyear, or semester, or even the week without going crazy.

Yet deep down inside, I knew I would not quit. My parents ingrained in me that you do not give up just because a task is difficult. You toughen up and move forward. At those moments during some of the most strenuous years of my journey, I had to find the determination to tackle the challenges in my path. I knew that in my weakness, God's strength would sustain me (2 Corinthians 12:10). So I chose to believe that I would reach my goals because of Him. Clinging to the encouragement from my mom and dad as well as from dear friends who reassured me that I could make it, I kept walking the road God had paved for my life (Hebrews 12:1). And ultimately, I never quit…even when I felt like it.

Now that my college days are behind me, I can assure you that my survival was merely the product of the following things: the God-given strength to fulfill His calling, the inspiration from family and friends to hang in there, and the grit that you choose to have in the face of life's toughest challenges. When you come to a rough spot on your journey, do not quit. If God has called you, know for sure that He will equip you (1 Thessalonians 5:24). Even in your weakest moments, your burden has not affected His power.

Simply ask God to strengthen you, and He will be your Help (Psalm 46:1). Likewise, you have to be determined...a half-hearted Christian will never spiritually survive the valleys. Resolve to stand, even when you feel like quitting (Ephesians 6:13-14). And then let me be that friend who encourages you to keep going. You can make it!

The Journey
of a
Lifetime

Chapter 10

A Teaching Masterplan

∽♪◑◠◔

If I could, I would write the plans today for the rest of my life. I like to know exactly what will happen and how every detail is going to work out. Some people are blessed with the ability to go with the flow and, as my daddy says, just play it by ear! That is *so* not my personality. I want everything prearranged way before the moment arrives. As a result, I write lists, create schedules, and even think of back-up plans. Waiting for last-minute details to fall into place nearly drives me crazy. I like to be prepared.

Let me give you a snapshot of my planning style. Several years ago, my grandparents were coming to meet us in Missouri for a summer vacation to celebrate my grandma's eightieth birthday, and I wanted to make sure we made it the best week possible. So I started brainstorming ideas, planning meals, researching local attractions, and organizing a schedule. Of course, I began months in advance. Perhaps I went a little overboard…you are welcome to your own judgement of that! But regardless, I almost enjoyed the preparation as much as I did the actual vacation.

My written schedule was so extensive that it included activities in chronological order for each day, detailed time-slots, and specific transportation arrangements. I also made sure to include when we would eat, what the food would be, and where we would have our meals. This was no last-minute, "What should we do today?" kind of trip. I wanted everything organized into the most efficient arrangement possible. When the special week finally arrived, we did not have to waste our play time figuring out an agenda. We jumped straight into a crammed vacation with a comprehensive schedule serving as our plan of attack. *Effective?*...absolutely! *Exciting?*...you had better believe it! *Extreme?*...maybe so. But in any case, I am a hard-core planner.

In 2012, I enrolled in an online university with the goal of becoming a credentialed teacher. I was well aware that this aspiration required a BS degree, an MAT degree, and a five-month internship. To be quite honest, the five years of college were not nearly as intimidating to me as the student teaching semester at the end of my program. I would have to stop traveling to teach at a school! That was scary. What state would I live in? Who would I stay with? What Christian academy would meet the university's requirements? I needed to begin planning early…or so I thought.

This would be an intense task even for a planner like me. I started trying to sort out my options. There were so many variables involved, and besides, a lot could change in a few years. A lot did change. As some possibilities seemed to fade while new options became available, I tried even harder to figure out the right ones. A finite mind, despite planning expertise, was just not capable of making the blueprint for my student teaching.

Frequently, my dad endeavored to convince me that my internship was still years or months away, and I did not need to worry about all the details because God had a plan. Let me say this. When you are the one giving this type of advice, it seems easy to accept. But when you are on the receiving end, it is much harder to fully embrace. I am not by any means justifying doubt. However, I am saying that as humans, we tend to set our faith on the back burner when it comes to making concrete plans for our lives. Too often we fail to calculate the divine into our equations. We forget that God is the most proficient Planner and that He knows what He is doing (Jeremiah 29:11). Seeking God's will is the best preparation for every stage of life's journey.

As I prayed for the Lord to open the doors

for my student teaching and tried to be sensitive to His direction, He was faithful to guide. Looking back now, I can see the miraculous finger of God orchestrating details for my internship before I ever began working on my graduate degree. Sometimes it is hard to imagine the entire picture when God is giving you one jigsaw piece at a time. But just wait till that puzzle is complete. Honestly, I never dreamed how amazing God's masterplan would be.

It was a chilly winter morning in January 2016. We pulled on our heavy jackets, climbed into our truck, and headed for a Christian school about ten miles down the road. Let me briefly fill you in. Our family was spending the week in Tennessee to record our first album. Meanwhile, I had heard about a local Christian academy where our producer's children attended.

Since my childhood idea of an elementary classroom was a trailer, a bus, or the cab of a pick-up, I wanted to get a glimpse of what a "normal" classroom looked like. Furthermore, I had never experienced an educator standing at the front of a grade-specific classroom and teaching a group of students who were sitting at individual desks. Within the next couple years, I would have to complete my student teaching in a traditional school, so I decided it was probably good for me to at least be familiar with this type of setting.

I can still remember walking into the sand-colored brick building for the first time. The guys had stayed in the truck while Momma and I went inside the schoolhouse. We received a warm greeting from the headmaster who readily welcomed us into his office. He asked us a few questions about our lives and my interest in Christian education. We explained that I was studying to be an elementary teacher and that, if at all possible, I was interested in seeing an elementary class in session.

When the headmaster wanted to know my preferred grade-levels, I told him second grade or third grade. Before Mom and I could fully grasp what was happening, the headmaster planned for me to eat lunch with the third-grade teacher and students in the cafeteria and then observe in the third-grade classroom for the remainder of the day. This was definitely more extensive than what my family and I had in mind. We assumed my first classroom experience would be just a few minutes of observation, and I would be accompanied by my mother. One of my greatest fears about student teaching was having to go into a school where I did not know anyone…and suddenly, I was having to face that fear much sooner than I anticipated. Regardless, we decided that the opportunity was too good to pass up, so we agreed to the plans.

The headmaster was more than happy to get me into the classroom right away. I said a quick goodbye to Momma, and my family left. All at once, I was alone in a very new environment. However, the teacher was so kind, and the students were friendly. Adjusting turned out to be easier than I thought. Toward the end of the school day, I had the opportunity to be down in the floor with the students, helping them at their learning stations. Honestly, I was already having a blast with the third-graders only a few short hours after I stepped onto the unfamiliar campus for the first time.

The school day seemed to close as abruptly as it began, so I was excited that the headmaster invited me to come back the following Monday to observe for the entire day. Soon, Mom arrived to pick me up. I will never forget our walk from the schoolhouse to our truck. In fact, I was barely out of the building when I started crying as I explained to Momma that I felt so at home in the classroom. I credited that exceptionally comfortable feeling to my passion for teaching. And perhaps, that was part of it. But I had no idea what God was planning behind the scenes.

What seemed so remarkable when I walked into the office on that brisk January morning was that I was a total stranger to everyone in the academy, yet for some reason, the Lord had given me favor. My family and I recognized that this was a God-ordained encounter with the school, the headmaster, and the third-grade teacher. However, we did not realize the major part this connection would play in my life during the months ahead.

As time passed and I continued seeking God's direction for my internship, the Tennessee school I had visited kept popping into my head. The more I thought and prayed about it, the more I was convinced that I was supposed to complete my student teaching at that Christian academy. However, there were several obstacles involved. At the other schools where I considered doing my student teaching, we had been connected with people in the area for at least a decade. I had friends or family who I could live with or near. And there were local churches we had ministered at where I could attend.

If I decided to teach in Tennessee, essentially, I would be moving into a completely new area. No long-standing relationships, no home to live in, no familiar church family…and really, my only connection with the school was 11 hours in the third-grade classroom and a 20-minute discussion with the headmaster. From a natural perspective, I had no grounded reason to believe that Tennessee was the place for me. As a result, I was hesitant to mention it to my parents because I assumed they would think I was crazy. To be blunt, my mom and dad had every right to that opinion because my hopes of teaching in Tennessee were a little outlandish.

I cannot think of a specific time when I broke the news to either of my parents that I wanted to complete my practicum in The Volunteer State at my dream school. It was almost like we all were on the same page. Even though we never sat down to have a discussion about the topic, we had individually been talking to the Lord. And He was giving each of us the same direction.

Then the door miraculously opened during September 2016 for me to fulfill my two-week practicum at that Christian academy in Tennessee. I decided that my practicum lent the perfect opportunity to ask the headmaster if he would consider allowing me to be placed in his school for my internship the following year. Around the time I was beginning the two-week field experience, my daddy unexpectedly asked me if I was going to talk with the headmaster about student teaching. I was surprised that my dad actually brought up the subject. To be honest, he absolutely did not like the idea of me having to come off the road for a semester. So, if Daddy was not giving me advice to pray and trust God about my student teaching, he usually brushed off the topic in a joking way. I was even more shocked that he too believed I was supposed to spend nearly five months in Tennessee to finish my education. In that unforgettable moment, I suddenly realized the first major phase of God's masterplan was beginning to unfold before my eyes.

The opening days of my practicum were a great learning experience for me, and everything seemed to be going smoothly. By Thursday evening, I resolved that it was time to email the headmaster to schedule a meeting with him. So I sent him a message to request an appointment. Friday morning after chapel, I was quietly filing out of the sanctuary along with the third-grade teacher and her students. To my surprise, when I passed by the headmaster, he told me that I could meet him in his office.

I became very nervous very quickly. This meeting was my opportunity to ask the headmaster if I could fulfill my internship requirements in his school. Talk about a lot of pressure and a giant knot in your stomach! If I did not say the right things, I could forfeit my chance to student teach at this Christian academy. Besides, Momma was not with me this time. I had to do *all* the talking myself...which is not normally an issue for me. However, this meeting was a crucial one, both for my education and for my future.

Right away, I texted my parents to have them pray. Then I slipped into a side room to ask the Lord to give me strength and favor and to guide my words. I had to come to the conclusion that if it was God's will, the headmaster would accept my request. If not, God had a better plan, and I would be content with whatever road He chose for me.

After arousing my courage, I walked through the open doorway of the office and took a seat in the brown leather chair across from the headmaster's desk. The scene itself was too sophisticated for my liking. But I had come too far to look back now. Besides, if there was no meeting, there would be no chance for the student teaching placement I dreamed of.

The headmaster was professional, yet remarkably kind. I briefly shared that I was interested in completing my student teaching at his school during the fall semester of the following year, but I clarified that I did not need an answer right away. When I said that he was welcome to pray about my request and then get back with me, his response was astounding. The headmaster assured me that he had already prayed about the situation and that he would be happy to grant my wishes. In fact, he even offered to fulfill the duty of on-site supervisor during my internship. I was amazed how quickly his side of the plans were settled. Honestly, our conversation was only a few minutes long. It seemed as if the Lord had been in that office before me, speaking directly to the headmaster.

Once I expressed that I would like my placement to be in the third-grade classroom, the headmaster instructed me to ask the third-grade teacher if she was willing to be my mentor. Then, simply email him the teacher's decision after I talked with her. As I walked down the hallway towards the classroom, I felt overwhelmed with joy. Yet somehow, I was even more afraid of the next step on my journey.

For the remainder of the school day, I thought about discussing my student teaching with the third-grade teacher. But even when the timing seemed perfect, I could not push myself to address the topic. Since I had another week to spend in the classroom with the third-grade teacher, I did not want her to feel pressured to say yes or awkward if she said no. I wanted her honest opinion. However, I did know that if I waited until the following week to speak with the teacher about my internship, I would be miserable the whole weekend. I cannot handle a half-made decision.

After school dismissed, we headed for the car pick-up line. The September air was chilly with intermittent rain. As a result, the elementary students were waiting in the building for their parents to arrive, and most of the teachers were inside supervising the children. However, I was standing outside under the awning with the third-grade teacher who had the job of helping students into their cars.

For a few minutes, we were alone, just us two...and I realized my opportunity was now. So I nervously expressed to the teacher the same thing I told the headmaster, also assuring her that I had already spoken with him about my internship. I explained that whatever response she gave me was completely okay and that she could feel free to pray about my request before giving me an answer. The words barely came out of my mouth when she eagerly agreed to be my mentor. It seemed too good to be true. I had been nervous for nothing.

The following Monday, I was once again amazed when the teacher clarified why she did not need to pray about my request. She had already been praying for me to do my student teaching with her! I could hardly wrap my mind around the things that were unfolding. God had been talking to everyone involved. Clearly, a third-grade classroom in a Tennessee Christian school was part of God's blueprint for my internship.

For a moment, let me jump ahead a few

months. It was the following spring when I got word that the headmaster of this Christian school in Tennessee was resigning from his position. He would no longer be on staff by the time I began my student teaching in the fall of 2017. At first, I felt very disappointed about this transition because the headmaster had been such an instrumental figure in my education. Then, I was overwhelmed with another thought. The headmaster would not have been at the school to arrange my student teaching if I had stretched out my graduate degree one more year like I originally planned. God's timing was evident, and His goal was clear. This unforeseen change of administration simply provided another confirmation of a divine masterplan.

My internship would be at the first classroom I ever stepped foot into, and my mentor teacher would be the same instructor who had welcomed me to my initial encounter with a regular school. I was thrilled to imagine the experience that awaited. God had miraculously organized every detail. In a single day, what once seemed like a giant barrier became a stepping stone on my journey.

But there was one more major question that needed an answer: Where would I live? Since we were not going to be back in Tennessee until my student teaching semester the following year, I was eager to nail down my new home before I finished my two-week practicum. However, the place I dreamed of living was even more far-fetched than the school where I wanted to teach. I rarely mentioned it to my parents. And when I did, I usually tried to make the comments really lighthearted because, in the natural, it was an unreasonable wish. I did not want it to appear that I was being irrational…but I just could not stop thinking about that family I wanted to claim as my own.

They traveled and sang southern gospel music like hundreds of other people do. But from the first time we saw them in concert, we could tell there was something special about them. Their love for God and heart for ministry were unmistakable. The Holy Spirit's anointing flowed through their singing. Extremely talented, yet remarkably humble. Their personalities were fun and loving. But ultimately, this family was genuine. Somehow, we just felt a connection.

Then everything fell into place to record our CD at their studio. It seemed that the Lord had allowed our paths to cross. Our families never had extended periods of time together that normally foster a strong relationship. But instead, many special moments characterized our short times together, and we began developing a friendship. I felt exceptionally close to them…as if we had been friends my entire life. Yet we were only with each other a few hours here and there. Regardless, we all seemed to recognize that our relationship was God-ordained.

This was who I wanted to stay with. To me, it would be perfect. The three daughters were amazing girls whom I absolutely loved. The parents were a wonderful man and woman of God who I felt like could be my adopted dad and mom. Besides, they lived in the same town as the school where I would be teaching, and their church where her brother pastored was only a few minutes away.

Strangely, my parents also started feeling a peace about the idea of me living with this family. However, we were absolutely not going to ask them. That would be a huge sacrifice to allow someone to live in their home, especially considering their ministry and busy lifestyle.

Although this family knew I would be student teaching at the school, we never said anything about me staying with them. Instead, we prayed for the Lord to speak to their hearts if it was His will. As crazy as it sounds, my momma specifically asked God for the mother to approach us about the situation. God had already done some talking to the headmaster and teacher at the school...so we were trusting Him to do the miraculous once again. Since our hopes appeared to be absurd, our only option was to pray and then leave it in God's hands.

The Sunday before Christmas 2016 was bitterly cold in southern Missouri. With daytime temperatures in the low teens, it was almost dreadful to be outside for very long. Wispy snow flurries were dusting the frozen countryside. We dressed in church clothes and then layered with boots, gloves, scarves, and wool coats to brave the cold. Soon we were off to an evening Christmas concert where our friends were scheduled to sing. It was going to be our last time together for several months because we were heading to California shortly after the holidays. We were anxious to see them, but it would be bittersweet.

After a fun reunion of hugs, stories, and laughter, we enjoyed a wonderful Christmas celebration with songs and treats of the season. Our friends ministered through soul-stirring melodies in a powerful fashion. When the concert was over, I stood behind the product table to hang with the girls and to help customers. Unexpectedly, the girls began telling me that I should come live with them the following year while I was student teaching. In a way, the conversation seemed so normal and yet it was unbelievable too. My reply was that they would have to talk to their momma. So they did…right there at the product table!

Once they brought up the idea to their mom, her reply to me was even more unreal. She said that I was welcome to live with them, but that I could pray about it first. I am not sure what my face looked like because I can be quite expressive without saying anything. But the thoughts racing through my mind were something along the lines of...*I cannot believe what I am hearing...My parents and I have been praying about this for the past six months...I am witnessing a miraculous answer to prayer right before my eyes.* Inside, I wanted to scream because I was way beyond excited. However, I replied calmly with a thank you so much, and I would speak about it with my parents.

Other than a few workers, the concert venue had completely emptied by the time we walked with our friends out to their bus in the frigid, night air. Goodbyes are never fun, especially when they mean a parting of ways for an extended time. Soon, the guys were loading the last pieces of equipment and having their final conversations. Momma and I were saying goodbye to this precious family's mom when she said, "We want Rachelle to come live with us when she does her student teaching." Tears started filling my eyes as I glanced over at my mom who looked as shocked as I did. Momma replied, "Are you serious?" I will never forget our dear friend putting one hand on my arm and the other on my mom's arm as if to emphasize her answer: "I'm serious." It was more than I could take in. We all exchanged warm smiles and hugs amidst the frosty, single-digit weather that engulfed us. The dream I once excused as my own wistful thinking was actually coming true...but in a more beautiful way than I could have imagined.

We needed to stop by our bus to pick something up and take it to our friends. So all of us left and then quickly reunited at a McDonald's parking lot just off the freeway. During our short drive, Momma and I had told my dad about our friends' invitation for me to live with them. None of us doubted that God had arranged this masterplan. As a family, we decided to tell them that we would accept their offer.

We stepped inside their bus to one of the most memorable experiences of my life. Two families crammed in just a few square feet...all of us standing close to hear a father-to-father conversation. The plans were confirmed. His words are etched in my mind: "I'll take your daughter." I was overwhelmed with gratitude and joy. My special friends who I admired and loved so much were going to be my second family. Not because we asked them...they asked us.

In fact, months later we realized that God had been speaking to their hearts as well. He was in touch with us and with our friends to communicate His will and to ensure its fulfillment. Truly, His divine masterplan for my student teaching was nothing less than a chain of miracles. This stretch of my journey that seemed so unclear during the previous four years was suddenly a well-lit path.

When I originally wanted to start planning my internship, I had never heard about the Christian school in Tennessee where I ended up teaching. The church I attended was not even existent yet. And we had only met the family who I lived with as a "famous gospel group" we loved listening to. At that time in my life, I would have never drawn up plans anything close to what God did. But He sees beyond our limited ideas to a world of possibilities that surpass our imagination.

The Lord has a purpose and a destiny for each one of His children. There are definitely moments along the way that you cannot see three feet in front of you. Rather than sitting in the dark, dare to trust that God's vision is much better than yours. Step out in faith. Be courageous (Deuteronomy 31:6). Know that the Lord never makes a mistake…in fact, He does everything well (Mark 7:37). Believe that if He made the plans, then He will walk with you to the finish line. God has a masterplan waiting for you. It is your decision whether or not you let Him guide your journey.

The Journey of a Lifetime

Chapter 11

Tennessee Girl

Recently, I was shopping in a home-décor store when I noticed a display of items, each decorated with paintings of vintage camp trailers. Of course, I am somewhat partial to homes with wheels, so I approached the shelves to browse through the trailer decorations. A sign caught my attention, which read, *Home is wherever we park it.* I smiled and thought, "Wow, that is the story of my life!" As simple as it may seem, I quickly realized that for me, the sign was more than a fun piece of décor to hang inside a camp trailer that hits the road several times a year for vacation. Instead, that sign portrayed an authentic motto for this evangelist girl. Although California was my birthplace and my state of residence for the first 12 months of my life, I have no memories of living there. Truthfully, home was always wherever we parked it. I knew nothing but life on the road, that is, until August 2017.

The final phase of my online college education was student teaching, a nearly five-month internship that had to be completed in a single location. I had watched God work countless miracles and open amazing doors to set the stage for my student teaching. Indeed, there was no doubt in my heart that I was in the middle of God's will by moving to Tennessee in August 2017. Though I was excited to travel the new stretch of my journey that lay ahead, I knew the adjustments involved would be drastic. Yet honestly, I do not think I fully grasped how drastic my transition would be, both for coming off the road and for leaving Tennessee to resume "bus life."

Feeling attached to a state, having a hometown, living in a stationary house, volunteering in a local church, following a normal daily routine, and driving alone are typical experiences for many people, but for this 23-year-old, such experiences were foreign. I could easily be in several states during the span of a few days, and "hometowns" changed more frequently than that. My house was only stationary when the transmission was in park. The local churches my family and I ministered in were only local to us for a week or so; then they quickly became distant mission fields once we had traveled the hundreds or thousands of miles to the next destination. Moreover, my daily routines were so diverse and unpredictable that I was quite afraid I would not know how to create or follow a normal one if it was ever necessary. Additionally, I had never even driven to the grocery store by myself. Student teaching was a much more extensive adjustment than transitioning from a college pupil to an elementary educator. The 2017 fall semester required a total renovation of nearly everything that was familiar to me, but I was eager to experience the changes that God had so carefully planned.

The weeks leading up to my student teaching were extremely busy as always, possibly even a little extra crammed. With barely any time to catch our breath, there was no preparation happening. In July, I spent two weeks finishing up my last intensive graduate courses in the hills of Virginia. During those weeks, I was stuck at the university campus for seven to nine hours every weekday, and then I waded through piles of homework and tutoring jobs in the evenings and on Saturday. Despite a packed schedule and a strenuous workload, I am always up for an adventure. And keep in mind, my idea of an adventure usually somehow involves music.

Since we had to be in Pennsylvania for a family photo shoot the morning after my second intensive course ended, we were planning to leave Virginia on Friday, immediately following my last class. As if those plans were not busy enough, I added an extra adventure to the agenda. Instead of our original schedule, my parents left early and took our bus to Pennsylvania on Friday morning. David kept our truck in Virginia, waiting for me to get out of class. My two-hour final seemed like a steep trek up a towering mountain, but clicking that submit button sure felt like I was dancing at the top. I was thrilled to bid farewell to that college campus. My brother and I jumped in our faithful means of transportation – the white Ford pick-up, complete with peeling paint and camouflage seat covers. Then, we were headed off to celebrate my achievement.

Our adventure led us on a planned detour through the winding roads of West Virginia. Some dear friends of ours were singing at an evening concert, and an extra three hours of driving is just a short jaunt for evangelist kids. In my opinion, an anointed southern gospel concert and time spent with friends are moments worth a drive. Besides, this was the last concert excursion for my brother and me before I moved out of the bus, so we were going to make the most of it! After some amazing music, fun fellowship, and a few more hours on the road, we climbed into bed between 3:00 and 4:00 AM. Of course, our 8:00 AM photo shoot came all too soon, especially since it was outdoors in the rain! I am sure by now you are convinced we are crazy, but I truly believe that this is our unstated philosophy: *The more activities we can pack into a 24-hour period, the more memories we will have for a lifetime.*

We continued living in the fast lane for the next two weeks leading up to my student teaching. When we left Pennsylvania en route to Tennessee, we were embarking on a one-day trip that would cover four states and a few hundred miles of freeway. However, I was ultimately beginning an excursion that would change my lifestyle for five months and impact my journey forever.

On August 5, two days before the Christian academy's school year began, my family and I crossed the Tennessee state line. I had not started packing a single piece of my belongings, and I did not even have a car to drive. Though these issues may seem insignificant to some, not being packed and not having a car were two of the most stressful things that could have happened to me as I began my student teaching semester. But we had been living in sixth gear for the past month; there had been no time for packing. Moreover, although we had tried for several months to prayerfully find a vehicle, nothing had worked out. Though so much for this stage of my life had fallen into place the previous year, so much was still undone less than forty-eight hours before I stepped into the classroom.

Quite honestly, I am the type of person to start preparing weeks, months, or even years before an event. I plan ahead; that is just my personality. Procrastination scares me. Waiting until the last minute to make a decision is stressful. As a result, sometimes I have a hard time waiting on God when He does not intervene in a situation or give clear direction when I want it. If Psalm 27:14 ("Wait on the Lord: be of good courage, and He shall strengthen thine heart: wait, I say, on the Lord.") was an assessment with a pass or fail grade, I would have failed miserably. Sometimes, I think the Lord does have me re-take the test of trust over and over because I keep failing on my end for the same reason: a lack of complete faith that God will move in His perfect timing.

I am ashamed to admit that I was still struggling with trusting God to provide a petty car and to help me get packed when He had already orchestrated a blueprint for my internship that was nothing shy of a divine masterplan. Yet one thing I have learned from all the times I have had to study and re-take the test of trust is that God never fails His side of the contract. In my own life, I have experienced what some dear friends sang as ad-lib to a song: "You may not know, just have faith,

God's got this!" As long as we will give God our problems, cares, and needs, He has everything under control. On the other hand, when we try to play tug-of-war with God, we cannot rest in knowing that "God's got this" because really, He only has a fraction of the rope. Ultimately, whether we understand the dilemma with our natural minds or feel completely in the dark, we must give the Lord our entire situation and trust the One Who never fails.

I had to reach the conclusion that I could not get prepared for my student teaching or figure out the whole car situation on my own. Trusting God to finish what He started was my only reasonable choice (Philippians 1:6). With that in mind, my mom and I began packing whenever I was home which was not too often considering school, church, and errands for getting settled in the area. We definitely packed in stages – not specific, organized sessions – just stages. My packing process would have been quite the amusing experience for an onlooker. I really did not know what I was doing; I had never moved out for five months, or at all for that matter! Regardless, I managed to get a majority of my things together by the time I was scheduled to move in the house with my second family.

The physical fatigue from the previous

month of a chaotic schedule caught up with me, and by Sunday, I had a cold. Then, Wednesday night at church I started losing my voice. Now I can deal with being sick, but losing my voice? That made me frustrated. If you know me, you know I love talking. Furthermore, spending seven hours a day in a classroom with 18 third-graders, I kind of had to talk! And besides, my whole purpose in coming to Tennessee was to complete my student teaching, a task I could not accomplish without a voice.

Friday morning, I could not even speak above a whisper. I had to text my situation to my mentor teacher who graciously allowed me to stay home. What a great way to start off the first week of an internship…lose my voice and miss a day of school. I was certainly not thrilled with the circumstances, but it was life. And having that day off did turn out to be a blessing in disguise. God knew this girl needed more time to pack and prepare for the new phase of my journey that lay ahead. Through this experience, I realized that what the devil means for harm, God can use for the benefit of His children.

Meanwhile, that first week, Dad would drop me off at school in the morning and then go car shopping. Once again, waiting on God and trusting His direction proved to be the best option, and the Lord helped my dad find a deal on a charcoal grey

Ford Focus. I was so excited about my first car when Daddy drove it into the campground where we had our bus parked. That Silver Bullet, as my father soon named it, was small, but not too compact. It was a blast to drive, comfortable to ride in, and easy to maneuver. Also, my car had a hatchback, allowing me to go shopping with my new sisters and not worry about space for our bags! And with a Sirius XM radio, I could listen to all the southern gospel music I wanted to on *enLighten.*

Here is the ironic side of the story. Before my student teaching began, I was worried sick about all the driving I would have to do on my own because I was not a very confident driver. I had been driving for six years. I had driven in all different states. And I had never been in an accident. Really, there was no legitimate reason for me to fret over the driving aspect of my internship. I just did not look forward to being my own chauffeur, but I had no choice. However, once I got behind the wheel of my Silver Bullet, you could not keep me off the highway. In fact, I had visited seven states and racked up my odometer to 10,000 miles by the time I moved back to the bus in December. Somehow, that evangelist urge to travel had transferred from growing up loving to be a passenger to jumping in the driver's seat and hitting the road any time I had the chance.

The first two weeks of my student teaching were a blur of preparing, moving, and transitioning. I was so thankful that my parents and brother were there to walk with me through the opening stretch of this new chapter in my life. We moved my belongings into my new bedroom. We navigated my new hometown. We spent time with my new family. We attended my new church together. I had been so busy, there was hardly time to think about the reality of what was happening.

My emotions were a rollercoaster. In a way, I was excited beyond words for the five months that lay ahead. Yet I was also trying to process the huge transition. Being away from my parents and brother and not being in full-time ministry were completely unfamiliar experiences for me. Also, I would be living in a stationary house and spending over thirty-five hours a week at an elementary school. Besides, my second family traveled and ministered, which meant I would have to spend some nights at home alone. Nothing would be the same as the only life I had ever known.

That final Friday evening, the goodbyes were difficult. There were plenty of tears. Early the next morning, Daddy, Momma, David, and the bus were leaving for North Carolina, but I was staying behind. This had never happened before. I *always* left when the bus did. Instead, I waved a final farewell, stepped into the empty house, and locked the door behind me. I had never spent a night alone...never in my life! It was a moment on my journey that is etched in my mind. At first, it seemed like I could flop down in a chair and cry. But then the peace that only God can give flooded my heart (Philippians 4:7). I realized that I had to be strong, but not on my own. God had chosen this road for me, and He would empower me for every aspect of the journey. There was no doubt in my mind that I was in God's will. So, I rested in knowing that the time I would spend as a Tennessee girl was part of His masterplan.

Everything was very different to me, yet somehow it all quickly felt like normal. I did my best to maintain a basic routine, despite the fact that my days were nearly too crammed for even a fast-paced schedule to organize. There was simply a lot of stuff to juggle. I had to be at school from 7:45 AM to around 3:20 PM. Then, there were college assignments, errands, laundry, and so on. Besides, I loved spending time with my second family, volunteering at my church, hanging with friends, and traveling to concerts. My planned bedtime of 10:45 PM was only met on a rare occasion. But I decided that this five-month experience was once in a lifetime, and I could catch up on sleep later. In fact, so many things happened during my stay in

Tennessee that it would be far too much for a written record. Rather, I will try to just share a few highlights.

Change can be tough, especially when it affects the core of who you are. But when someone with genuine love locks arms with you and walks you through your valley, despair is turned to delight. Suddenly on your journey, the surrounding lowlands seem decorated with colorful flowers while glittering sun rays peek through the overhanging clouds. For me, that special someone was my new family who welcomed me into their home. I could not have survived those five months of change without my second dad and mom and three amazing sisters who filled my heart with joy and impacted my life forever.

Having sisters was an entirely new experience that I absolutely loved. The girls and I often stopped by Target for last-minute shopping sprees. And we frequented the Chic-fil-a drive-thru because nothing satisfies hunger pains like waffle fries and chicken nuggets. There were late nights for playing games, visiting, and having sleepovers. One evening, my youngest two sisters had their cousins over. Since all four of the girls wanted to try their hand at styling my hair, I sat on a chair in the bedroom and split my hair into four sections so each beautician could brush and braid together.

Days were adorned with sunglasses, music, slime production, hoverboards, shopping, cooking, cleaning, gym time, and such. Then there was the trip to Dollywood for concerts and rollercoaster rides. The makeshift car wash on the front lawn to clean my Silver Bullet. The family dinner around a candle-lit table set with country blue and white china. I have plenty of stories for each of these, just not enough pages.

Some nights, an amazing aroma filled the house and lured me downstairs to the kitchen in my pajamas and robe. There I would find homemade biscuits baked in a cast iron skillet…I can almost taste those nostalgic, fluffy treats that no one could make like my second dad. A slab of butter, a scoop of jelly, and a glass of milk were the perfect fixings to complete the snack. As winter approached, I discovered that my second family loves Christmas as much as I do. Listening to Christmas records, garnishing the front doorway with evergreen garland, setting the table with Christmas dishes, frosting sugar cookies, building a gingerbread house, and stringing rainbow-colored, blinking lights are treasured holiday memories from my Tennessee home.

One thing that did not change with my transition to Tennessee life was the pressure of online graduate school. The piles of college assignments felt higher than ever, and my professor was one of the most annoying instructors at the university. Yet the sand-colored brick schoolhouse that welcomed me every weekday was a constant reminder of God's favor and divine masterplan. My cooperating teacher was more than a caring mentor and a professional educator, she was my friend. I felt blessed beyond words to work with her in her classroom. All 18 energized third-graders made schooldays interesting. Of course, the kids were not perfect, but they were fun to teach and easy to love. From the field trip and craft projects to the cafeteria and car pick-up line, the memories are special.

At first, I was very insecure about my ability to be the primary instructor. However, as the semester progressed, I felt more comfortable at the front of the classroom than I ever imagined possible. I give the credit to the Lord Who enabled me and to my amazing cooperating teacher who cheered me on. My dream to complete student teaching at this Tennessee Christian school became a wonderful reality.

Weekends were often my time for adventure. Even though I had college work and laundry calling my name, I tried to always plan something that gave me a break from the daily grind. When my friends were singing at a weekend concert within a four-hour drive, I would pack a snack bag, set my phone's GPS, jump into my Silver Bullet, and go hear some southern gospel music. A couple times, I drove to Indiana for the weekend to be with my family in revival. One of those trips I kept as a secret between Mom and me to surprise my dad. It required some fenagling because Daddy was constantly checking in on me, asking about my weekend plans, and watching my location on his app. But as he walked into the bus after service and saw me sitting on the couch, he was absolutely shocked…mission accomplished!

My first time on a plane by myself was a weekend trip to New Jersey to visit my family and surprise my dear friends at their Friday night youth rally. Everything went smoothly except the initial flight delay caused by a cattle truck that wrecked on the freeway, spilling cows across the interstate and holding up my pilots in the traffic jam. For another memorable weekend, I went on the road with my second family. It was an awesome "bus life" fix amidst five months of living in a house. In less than forty-eight hours, we attended three church services, covered about 600 miles, and enjoyed some southern cooking at Lambert's Cafe. Yet regardless of where I traveled on the weekends, this die-hard Tennessee girl loved coming back home.

My life as an evangelist's daughter had been

wrapped up in full-time ministry, and coming off the road put a temporary end to that part of me. However, attending a home church was a new experience that found a special place in my heart. I loved referring to *my church* and *my pastors*...and I still do. Since I wanted to get the full effect of being involved, I decided to volunteer as a greeter. Quickly, I discovered that this basic aspect of ministry was so fulfilling, and it became my passion. I looked forward to the days I was scheduled to greet because I enjoyed interacting with fellow church members and visitors, and I cherished the idea of serving in my local church. As the harvest festival outreach approached, I was eager to take part in that church function. I helped with set-up and clean-up, supervised one of the games, and tasted pot after pot of chili to help judge who would win the chili cook-off. The truth is, I knew God had placed me in that church for that season of my life. My desire was to work for the Kingdom in any way I could.

Each week, I could not wait for Sundays and Wednesdays to roll around so I could be with my church family, hear my pastor preach, and spend time in God's presence. The altar services were very dear to my heart. They were opportunities for me to get spiritually recharged. They were moments when I could touch Heaven about the cares of life. They were special times of prayer with friends as we interceded for each other, for our church, and for America (James 5:16).

I will never forget the Wednesday night that my pastor had the congregation stand hand-in-hand and encircle the sanctuary. He led us in a powerful time of prayer, asking for the glory of God to fall both in our church and in our nation. I was standing between the pastor's brother and sister whose anointed ministries have reached more people in a decade than I probably ever will in my lifetime. Inspired by their lives and humbled by their Kingdom accomplishments, I felt blessed to agree in prayer with these stalwarts of the faith for revival to break out. As we were nearing the end of the altar service, Pastor charged the congregation to encourage each other that we are all needed in the Lord's work. Unexpectedly, I felt a hand rest on my shoulder. When I turned, my pastor's brother intently looked me in the eye, and with a gentle yet serious tone he said, "The Lord has need of you." Then for another second or two, he kept looking down at me and left his hand in a firm grasp on my arm as if to say, *I mean it.* This simple yet stirring moment sunk deep into my heart.

To think that God wanted me as a servant in His harvest field...I held a seemingly unimportant role in my church; I was just a greeter. And even in my 22 years of traveling, I could not boast grand religious accomplishments or testify that my life had reached the world for Christ. In comparison with this man's past and current ministry to thousands around the globe, my work for the Lord seemed trivial.

Nevertheless, the Bible is clear that God does not have favorites (Acts 10:34). His decision to use someone in ministry is not based on fame or talent. Rather, the Master uses those who have a heart for Him and a desire to fulfill His destiny for their lives (Acts 13:22). Sometimes it is easy to feel insignificant, especially when you meet people who have done so much for God. But the truth is, none of us are sufficiently equipped for ministry on our own. We are ineffective without the Holy Spirit's anointing. However, if we will allow God to work through us, there is no limit to what we can accomplish for His kingdom.

As my student teaching semester came to a close, I faced another difficult transition – moving out of my house and back to the bus. Of course, I was very excited to reunite with my parents and brother. Also, I felt sure that my return to full-time ministry on the road was God's plan for me. But I was extremely attached to my new family, my house, my church, and my state. I felt at home there. Besides, I had eagerly looked forward to my internship ever since God's masterplan unfolded the year before. Now, this miraculous phase of my journey had ended, and the experience I dreamed about had quickly turned into a cherished memory. The final weekend at my house, the last service at my church, and the goodbyes to my second family were all stained with tears. Even the few weeks that followed were an emotional struggle as I readjusted. Although "Tennessee girl" would no longer be my location description, it had become a part of my identity.

Just as the Lord strengthened me for the initial transition to a completely new lifestyle, He gave me the grace to step into the next chapter as well. Yes, I am back on the road and loving it. Full-time ministry is my passion. The black bus is home again, and I have no doubt that my calling is still to be an evangelist's daughter. But regardless of where my journey leads, I will always be a Tennessee girl.

The Journey
of a
Lifetime

Chapter 12

Trusting His Path

One winter Sunday evening while I was living in Tennessee, I attended a Christmas concert in Indiana about 150 miles away from home. After enjoying the stirring holiday tunes and visiting with dear friends, I climbed alone into my Silver Bullet. As usual, I set my phone's GPS, this time double checking the route to make sure I would be traveling home the most direct way. On a previous trip, I had chosen the route I wanted to take, and somehow after I started driving, the GPS decided to readjust my course. I was not going to take any chances of that happening again. When I was confident that my GPS was leading me correctly, I started off on another one of my frequent late-night excursions.

Once I was on the road, I decided to call and talk with my grandma so we could share stories and keep each other company. It was already December, but my busy college schedule and student teaching semester had only allowed me to spend a few days out of the whole year with my 82-year-old grandma. And since she lives far away from all her children and grandchildren, sometimes she gets lonely to see her family. To be honest, I was somewhat lonesome too since my only passenger on the trip was a snack bag!

Anyways, my grandma and I were deep in conversation when I noticed an incoming call from my dad. I quickly sent him a text to inform him that I was not answering his call because I was on the phone with my grandma. However, my text accomplished nothing. Instead, Daddy kept calling me until I finally interrupted my grandma to tell her that I needed to hang up and take my dad's call.

Let me note that every time I went on a trip, my dad would intently watch my progress on his phone using our location sharing app. Thus, when I answered the phone, my dad frantically told me that I needed to pull over immediately because I was going the wrong way! To make matters worse, my gas tank was nearly empty, and I would not make it to a gas station if I continued in the direction that my GPS was leading. Daddy instructed me to make a U-turn, and then he gave me some specific directions concerning the roads I needed to take. I quickly obeyed. Although my GPS stubbornly took a little while to readjust to the appropriate route, I made it to a gas station without having to push my car. Despite 30 minutes of waisted time and the hassle of getting off course, I was safely on my way home again. Looking back, I realized that sometime after I left the church parking lot, my GPS had decided it would take me a "better route" that would have eventually left me stranded.

When I initially moved to Tennessee, my dad advised me that even when I was following the GPS, I should always know the main road names and freeways I needed to take *before* I began the trip. That way, if something happened to the GPS, I could still stay on track. Unfortunately, the fateful evening in Indiana, I had skipped that preparation because I was in a hurry to get on the road, and I trusted the GPS.

Interestingly, I noticed that after I had been driving a little while, the area did not really look familiar. Some of the landmarks that I remembered from my drive to the concert were not where I thought they should be. However, I was busy talking to my grandma, and I reassured myself that surely the GPS knew the correct route home. Ultimately, I could have avoided going the wrong direction if I had applied my dad's advice, and I could have turned around sooner, not wasting as much time, if I had heeded the warning signs. Disregarding wise instructions, allowing actions to be distractions, and overriding uneasy feelings were choices that produced a frustrating and unfortunate situation during my trip. Likewise, these choices can be key ingredients for much worse failure and disaster in many aspects of our journey through life.

When someone or something you have trusted leads you astray, you can more fully grasp the significance of Proverbs 3:5-6... "Trust in the Lord with all thine heart; and lean not unto thine own understanding. In all thy ways acknowledge Him, and He shall direct thy paths." Christ is the only reliable GPS for our journey through life. He will never tell you to make a turn or take a road that will harm your walk with Him. When God gives directions, be obedient. He knows the best route home. Do not get distracted by relationships, desires, tragedies, rejection, or discouragement. If you happen to start going the wrong way, do not override the Holy Spirit's conviction. He is trying to help you realize that you are driving off the path. Be willing to ask God for forgiveness, make a U-turn, and move forward on the right road. Let me assure you, when He directs your path, you could never plan a more efficient, exciting journey.

The road will get rough or scary at times, but keep listening to God's voice. You may not understand everything, but that is okay; God never promised we would. In fact, if we had it all together on our own, we would not need a Guide. Simply place your complete trust in Heaven's GPS. He will not leave you stranded.

Through the years, I have witnessed God's faithfulness to my parents as they have endeavored to trust Him with their lives, ministry, and family. Even when the road was unclear, the skies were dark, and the situations seemed impossible, God came through. Now I have reached a point in my life that I have had to trust the Lord myself. Plans and problems relating to college, student teaching, and ministry taught me the importance of trust and the dependability of God during my own journey. In all these areas, my parents were praying with me for God's will to be accomplished, but the issues were on my shoulders too.

Then living in Tennessee, miles away from my family, I really had to know how to trust God on my own. Relying on godly parents is a blessing, but eventually, trust has to become a personal decision of total reliance on the Master. I definitely cannot say that I have reached a place where I never struggle with trusting God. There are days when I let doubt creep in. Nevertheless, I have learned that any time I mingle trust with reservation, I am hindering myself. There no legitimate reason to mistrust God, nor any evidence that He will fail. Quite honestly, I have no idea what the rest of my life will hold, but I am in this journey for the long haul. By trusting the One Who sees the future, I can overcome or accomplish whatever is around the next bend in the road.

At times along the journey, the Lord brings individuals into our lives, and there is no doubt they are Heaven-sent. Perhaps they are instrumental in sharing advice, giving financially, providing encouragement, or simply being a friend. But regardless of the part they play, it seems that those people are first-hand illustrations of Proverbs 27:17… "Iron sharpeneth iron; so a man sharpeneth the countenance of his friend." One such connection I experienced was a God-ordained encounter with a minister who quickly became a dear friend and even played a fatherly role in my life. His personality was so gentle, yet so compelling. His strong character and grounded beliefs were distinct, yet somehow, he could communicate advice in such a tender, uplifting way. Looking back, I can clearly see that the crucial timing of this friendship was truly part of God's plan.

During one of our conversations, my friend inspired me in a way that I will never forget. The experience is etched in my memory. We were at a large event center, sitting beside each other near the back wall of the auditorium. The music and surrounding noise was considerably loud, but we had managed to tune out the distractions. My friend's serious countenance and fatherly tone conveyed that he meant business, and his glossy black suit jacket with a dark paisley design added to his professional appearance.

While encouraging me to fulfill every aspect of God's calling and to branch into new avenues of ministry, he could sense I was apprehensive about moving forward in a specific area. My friend responded by lovingly yet bluntly explaining that the richest place on earth is the graveyard. All too often, it is filled with wasted lives, discarded talents, unwritten books, and unsung songs because people did not fully pursue the destiny God had planned for them. As tears streamed down my face, I determined that no matter what God asked me to do or what that commitment cost me, my grave would not be rich with unused energy, abilities, zeal, love, or dedication. At that moment, I resolved to go to the grave empty, having given my all for the cause of Christ and having trusted His path for my journey of a lifetime.

The Journey of a Lifetime